*Christian
Art
from its Origins
to the
Fifteenth Century
with
Illustrations
by
Thierry Bondroit
Odette Mukherjee
Joseph Schlipf
&
Hanna Losowska*

CLIP ART OF THE CHRISTIAN WORLD

*Christian
Art
from its Origins
to the
Fifteenth Century
with
Illustrations
by
Thierry Bondroit
Odette Mukherjee
Joseph Schlipf
&
Hanna Losowska*

edited by

BROTHER AELRED-SETON SHANLEY

PUEBLO PUBLISHING COMPANY
NEW YORK

The illustrations in this book
were first published
by Rizzoli International Publications, Inc., in
*Art of the Christian World, A. D. 200-1500:
A Handbook of Styles and Forms*
by Yves Christe, Tania Velmans, Hanna Losowska, and
Roland Recht.
® 1982 Office du Livre.

The illustrations are by Thierry Bondroit, Odette Mukherjee,
Joseph Schlipf and Hanna Losowska.

Copyright ® 1990 Pueblo Publishing Company, Inc.,
New York, New York

ISBN 0-925127-04-3

Printed in the United States of America

CONTENTS

*This
book
is dedicated
to the memory
of
Gary V. Girard
artist/designer
&
brother
pilgrim*

FOREWORD

An unusual quality of this book, though I am sorry that it should be unusual, comes from the fact that Christian art reaches far back before the schism between the Eastern and Western churches. In this anthology the titles of the feasts and many of the images remind us of our common tradition. I have included liturgical texts and chants that celebrate the Christian year from both the Eastern and Western Churches.

How we pray—and the images we use in prayer, especially in our liturgical prayer— say much about what we believe. In this regard, even as I assembled this book, I could not help but think of the many voices of women within the churches today. As powerful and wonderful as are the images presented here of the Pantocrator and the Face of Christ, I couldn't help but be impressed by the overpowering maleness of this collection — the many images of the Mother of God notwithstanding. The Mystery of the Incarnation necessarily is gender-specific at the level of historical narrative, yet surely this is only to take us beyond gender, deep into the heart of God, "beyond every name" as the letter to the Philippians points out. Yet Tradition also offers us images which have almost been lost in the West. I am thinking of the Myrrh-Bearing Women at the Tomb (*pp. 68-71*) who figure so prominently in the Paschal liturgy and iconography of the Eastern Church. These witnesses to the empty tomb are the first to proclaim the good news, yet our Roman liturgical texts —even after Vatican II— are often more concerned to call Peter the proto evangelist. I still remember a wonderful Carolingian manuscript illumination, (sadly not part of this anthology) depicting Mary of Magdala fearlessly proclaiming the Resurrection to a rather timid assembly of the apostles! This book celebrates the heritage of fifteen centuries: it can't begin to anticipate the images that may be borne of faith and Sophia in our time.

The catholic quality of this book, which embraces so many different expressions of the Christian artistic/theological endeavor ("faith seeking understanding"), gives this anthology both its strengths and its limitations as clip-art. The Church's Tradition is fascinated with certain images and neglects others. The collection here is especially strong in the Christmas and Easter Cycles. The Crucified Christ and Christ Pantocrator (the Cosmic Christ, whom Matthew Fox asks us to rediscover), appear in endless variety, as well as Mary, Mother of God / Theotokos, who is almost always shown with the infant.

There is a further limitation: the wonderfully varied renderings offered here were originally published in a handbook of Christian styles. The artists who chose the images for that book were not concerned with the feasts and seasons of the Church year but with giving a representative selection of Early Christian, Byzantine, Romanesque, Gothic and Renaissance art. Had they been commissioned to prepare this book for us, the collection here would look quite different.

I have had to work within these limitations. The beauty of the original masterworks, and the sometimes stunning quality of these contemporary renderings, seem to make such limits unimportant. I hope you enjoy using this book as much as I have enjoyed assembling it.

Brother Aelred-Seton
Hermitage of the Dayspring
Kent, Connecticut

EAF THROUGH these pages even briefly, and you will see that this is a most unusual book. While it is offered as a resource for graphic clip-art, a visual anthology that speaks of the Christian faith of women and men spanning fifteen hundred years is surely more than utilitarian. As you clip and paste —or simply page through this anthology for your pleasure— join your faith to those who first wrought these images and in turn let their faith enrich you and your communities.

In order to encourage a more reflective approach to using this collection, I have included, here and there, brief texts drawn from an immense variety of sources. I hope they will speak to that Mystery which Saint Paul says is "Christ-in-us." They are primarily intended for you, though they too could be employed as clip-art when appropriate.

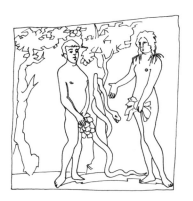

*Only
all these
thousand
and one
human
varieties,
who in
cooperation
or in conflict,
form the one
course
of world
history,
together
bring to
realization
what
was really
intended
when God
said in the
beginning:
"Let us make
human beings
in our
image and
likeness."*

KARL RAHNER

*God's
relationship
with human
beings
started
by renouncing
power
over them.*
adapted from
KARL STERN

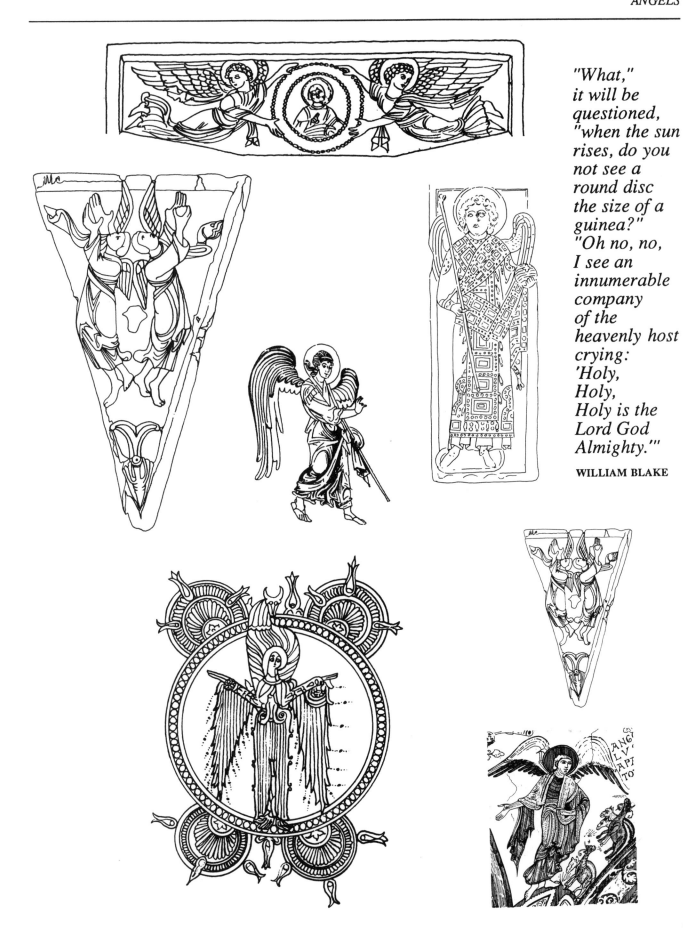

"What,"
it will be
questioned,
"when the sun
rises, do you
not see a
round disc
the size of a
guinea?"
"Oh no, no,
I see an
innumerable
company
of the
heavenly host
crying:
'Holy,
Holy,
Holy is the
Lord God
Almighty.'"

WILLIAM BLAKE

*No evil
shall
ever
befall
you,
no danger
descend on
your house
for
God's angels
have all been
charged
to guard you
wherever
you go.*
PSALM 91

*The
"Thy will
be done,"
the
unconditional
Yes
which we
pronounce
every day
in prayer
and
which
leads to a
thousand little
incarnations,
at one
central
moment
in history,
led to the
Incarnation.*

KARL STERN

*Moment
of
unequalled
faith,
here
in any time
or place–
thus
did God
put on
our flesh
in a Virgin
full of grace.*

STANBROOK HYMNAL

*You are built
upon
the foundation
laid
by the apostles
and prophets,
and
Christ Jesus
himself
is the
foundation
stone.
In him
the whole
building
is bonded
together
and grows
into
a holy temple
in the Lord.*

EPHESIANS 2:20-22

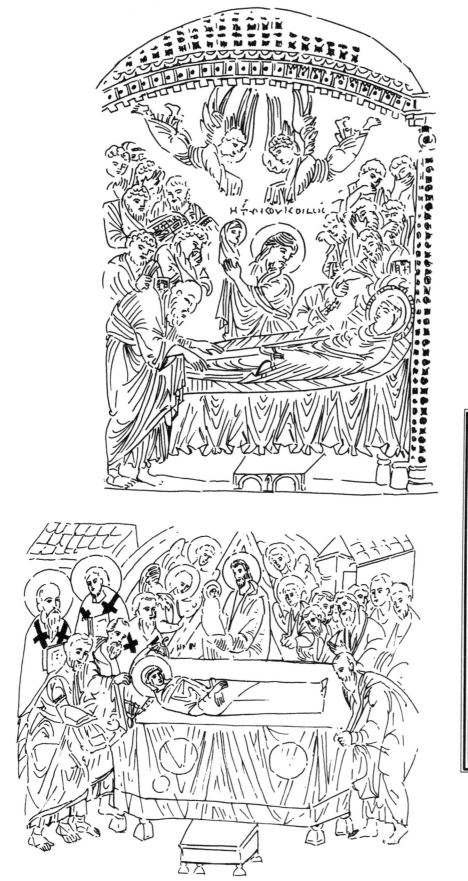

*Maiden,
yet a Mother,
Daughter
of thy Son,
High
beyond all
other—
Lowlier is none;
Thou
the
consummation
Planned
by
God's decree,
When
our lost creation
nobler rose
in thee!*

**DANTE
trans. Ronald Knox**

*Unless
we cultivate
sensitivity
to the
Glory
while here,
unless
we learn how
to experience
a foretaste
of heaven
while on earth,
what
can there be
in store for us
in life to come?
The seed
of eternal life
is planted
within us
here and now.*
ABRAHAM HESCHEL

*Love
the poor
and infirm,
strangers
and
the homeless.
Encourage
the faithful
to work with you
in your
apostolic task;
listen willingly
to what they
have to say.
Never relax
your concern
for those who
do not yet
belong to the
one fold of
Christ.
They too are
commended
to you
in the Lord.*

**RITE
OF CONSECRATION
OF A BISHOP**

*What shall
we offer you,
O Christ,
who have
appeared
to us
on earth,
taking on
our flesh?
Every one
of your creatures
-your
handiwork-
offers you
its thanks:
The angels
sing their hymns;
the heavens
offer a star;
the magi
bring their gifts;
the shepherds,
their wonder;
the earth,
its cave;
the wilderness,
a manger:
and we,
we offer you
a Virgin Mother!
O God
from everlasting,
have mercy on
us.*

ORTHODOX CHANT

18

...mind
without soul
may blast
some
universe
to might have
been
and stop
ten thousand
stars
but not one
heartbeat
of this child;
nor shall
even prevail
a million
questionings
against the
silence
of his mother's
smile
—whose
only secret
all
creation
sings

e. e. cummings

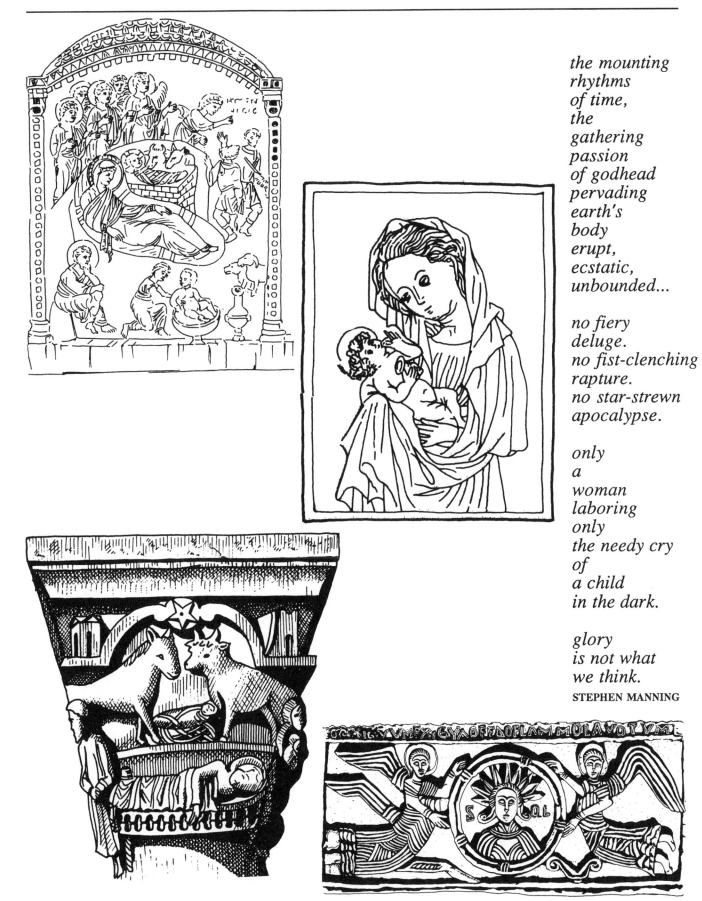

the mounting
rhythms
of time,
the
gathering
passion
of godhead
pervading
earth's
body
erupt,
ecstatic,
unbounded...

no fiery
deluge.
no fist-clenching
rapture.
no star-strewn
apocalypse.

only
a
woman
laboring
only
the needy cry
of
a child
in the dark.

glory
is not what
we think.

STEPHEN MANNING

*...can we begin
to comprehend
this myst'ry
nursing
Mary's breast
who
challenges
our human
hopes;
who never more
will give us
rest?*

**THE DAYSPRING
HYMNAL**

God allows
himself
to be edged out
of the world
and onto
the cross.
God is weak
and powerless
in the world,
and that is
exactly the way,
the only way,
in which God
chooses
to be with us...
Human
religiosity
makes us look
in our distress
to the power
of God
in the world...
The Bible,
however,
directs us to the
powerlessness
and suffering
of God—
only
a suffering God
can help.

DIETRICH
BONHOEFFER

O dying souls,
behold
your
living spring;
O dazzled eyes,
behold
your
sun of grace;
Dull ears, attend
what word
this Word
doth bring;
Up, heavy
hearts,
with joy
your joy
embrace.
From death,
from dark,
from deafness,
from despairs,
This life,
this light,
this Word,
this joy repairs.

ROBERT SOUTHWELL

*Gold
long had gilt
the courts
of kings
and incense
gave the gods
delight;
but myrrh
was bitter,
—deemed
for death—
and shed
on these
a different
light....*
**THE
DAYSPRING HYMNAL**

*Jesus goes up
out of the water;
for in himself
he carries up
the whole world
and sees
the heavens
split open
which Adam
had shut up
against
himself and all
his posterity...
and the Spirit
descends...
and like a dove
seen in bodily
form
it bestows
honor
on his body
since this
is also God
by being
deified.*
GREGORY NAZIANZEN

One
does not
become
enlightened
by imagining
figures
of light
but by
making
the darkness
conscious...
CARL JUNG

Today
the Church
has been
wedded
to her heavenly
bridegroom,
for Christ
has washed her
sins in the
Jordan:
the Magi
hasten
with their gifts
to
the royal
Wedding,
and the wedding
guests
are made merry
for water
is turned
into wine!

**ANTIPHON
TO THE BENEDICTUS:
FEAST
OF THE EPIPHANY**

*All
being
is
nuptual.*

KARL STERN

*The
commonplace
is charged
with life!
A wedding feast
becomes
a sign:
Christ weds
the peoples
of his heart
while
changing
water into wine!*

**THE
DAYSPRING HYMNAL**

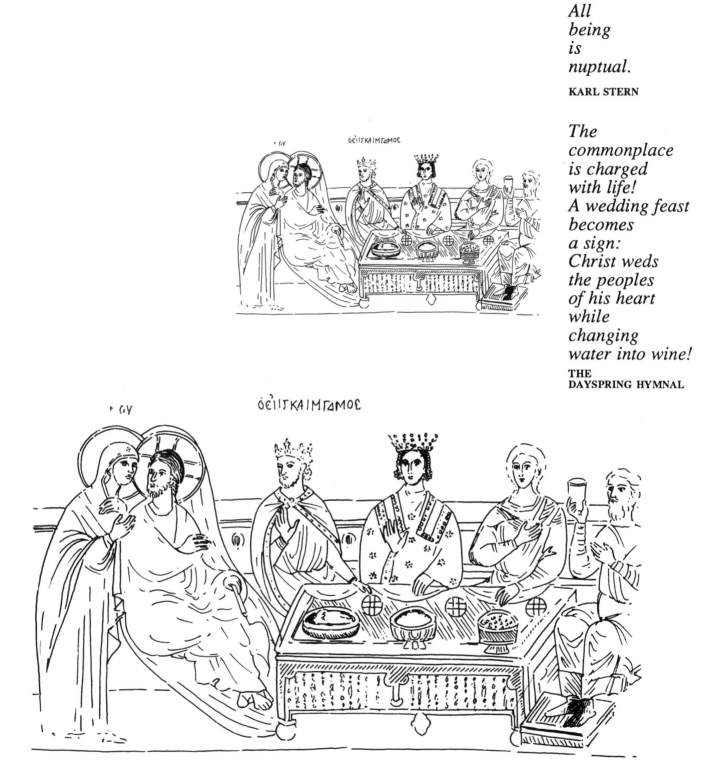

*Our
destination
is
never
a place,
but
rather
a new way
of looking
at things.*
HENRY MILLER

...the child
is saved
by flight
"to Egypt."
Jesus
relives
not only
the Exodus
of Israel
"from Egypt,"
but also,
and first,
the departure
of Israel from
Canaan into
Egypt.
RAYMOND BROWN

*How
can I begin
to repay
all the Lord's
gifts
to me?
I will raise
the cup
of salvation
and
invoke
the Lord's
name.*
PSALM 116

The whole world is your temple, shaped to resound with your name. Yet you also allow us to dedicate to your service places designed for your worship.

PREFACE: RITE OF DEDICATION OF A CHURCH

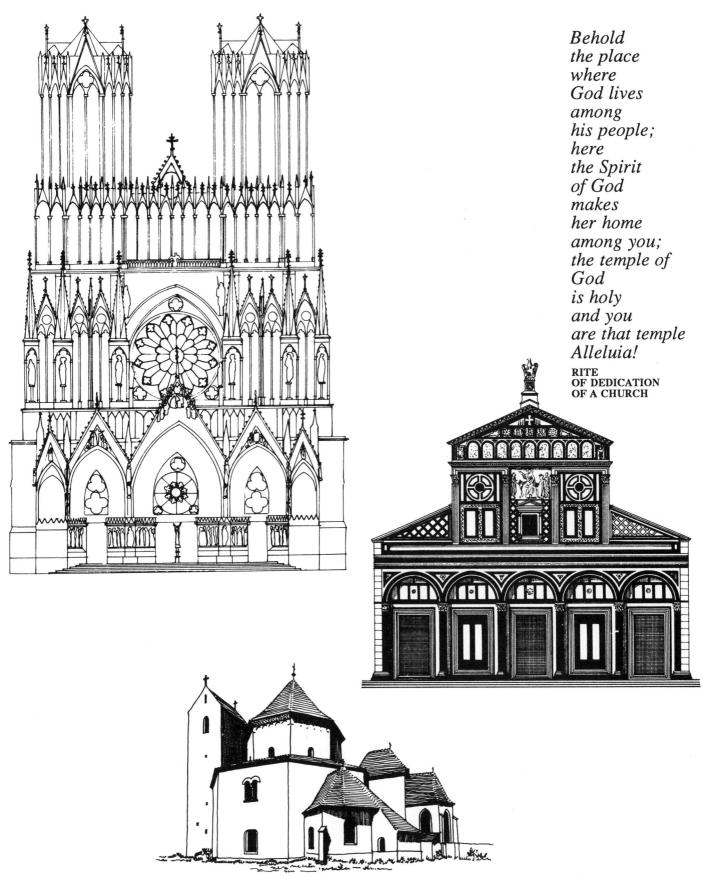

*Behold
the place
where
God lives
among
his people;
here
the Spirit
of God
makes
her home
among you;
the temple of
God
is holy
and you
are that temple
Alleluia!*

**RITE
OF DEDICATION
OF A CHURCH**

Only in me, in my faith, in my life & in my action can the Cross of Christ become life and power. For in the Christian faith, the world is not an "idea," an abstract and impersonal "totality," but always the unique gift to a unique human being. The world given to me, by God as my life & my vocation, my calling, my work, my responsibility. No idea, no doctrine can save the world, yet it perishes, or is saved in each person.
And it is saved each time one accepts the Cross and one's own "crucifixion unto the world."

ALEXANDER SCHMEMANN

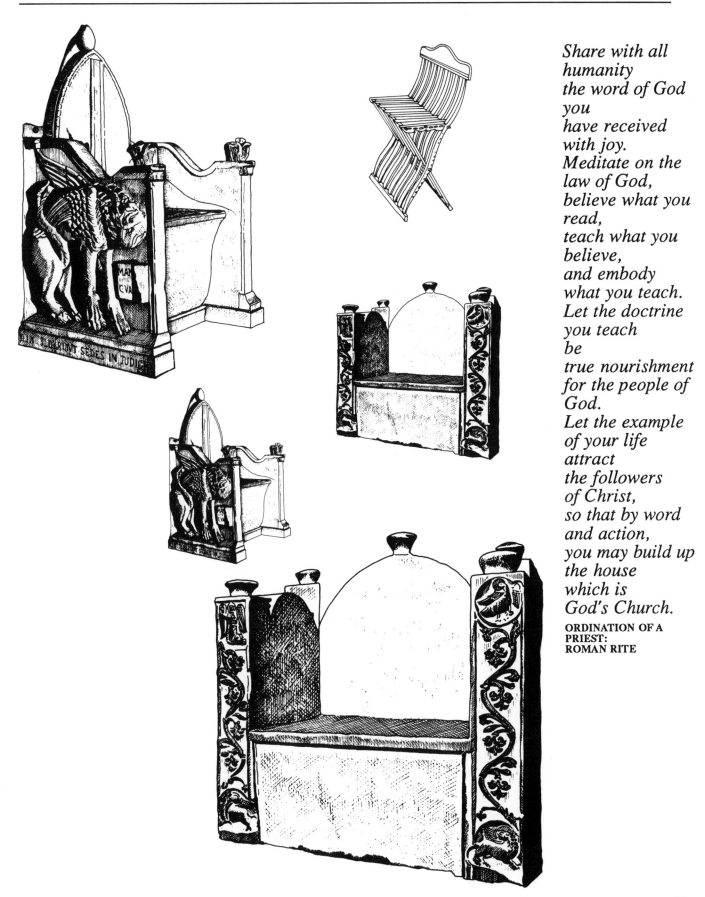

Share with all humanity the word of God you have received with joy. Meditate on the law of God, believe what you read, teach what you believe, and embody what you teach. Let the doctrine you teach be true nourishment for the people of God. Let the example of your life attract the followers of Christ, so that by word and action, you may build up the house which is God's Church.

ORDINATION OF A PRIEST: ROMAN RITE

*...Make it
a table of joy,
where
the friends of
Christ
may hasten
to cast
upon you
their burdens
and cares
and
take up their
journey
restored....*

**DEDICATION OF AN
ALTAR:
ROMAN RITE**

*Rejoice,
heavenly
powers!
Sing,
choirs
of angels!
Exult,
all creation
around
God's
throne!
Jesus Christ,
our King,
is risen!
Sound the
trumpet
of salvation!
Rejoice,
O earth,
in shining
splendor,
radiant in the
brightness of
your king!
Christ has
conquered!
Glory fills you!*

**THE EASTER
PROCLAMATION**

*Through
Christ
God chose
to reconcile
the whole
cosmos
to himself,
making peace
through
the shedding
of his blood
upon the cross—
to reconcile
all things,
whether on earth
or in heaven,
through Christ
alone.*

COLOSSIANS 1:20

*Use this
visible
creation as it
should
be used,
as you use the
earth,
sky, air, springs,
and rivers.
And whatever
is beautiful and
wonderful
in them
acknowledge
to the praise
and glory
of God.*

LEO THE GREAT

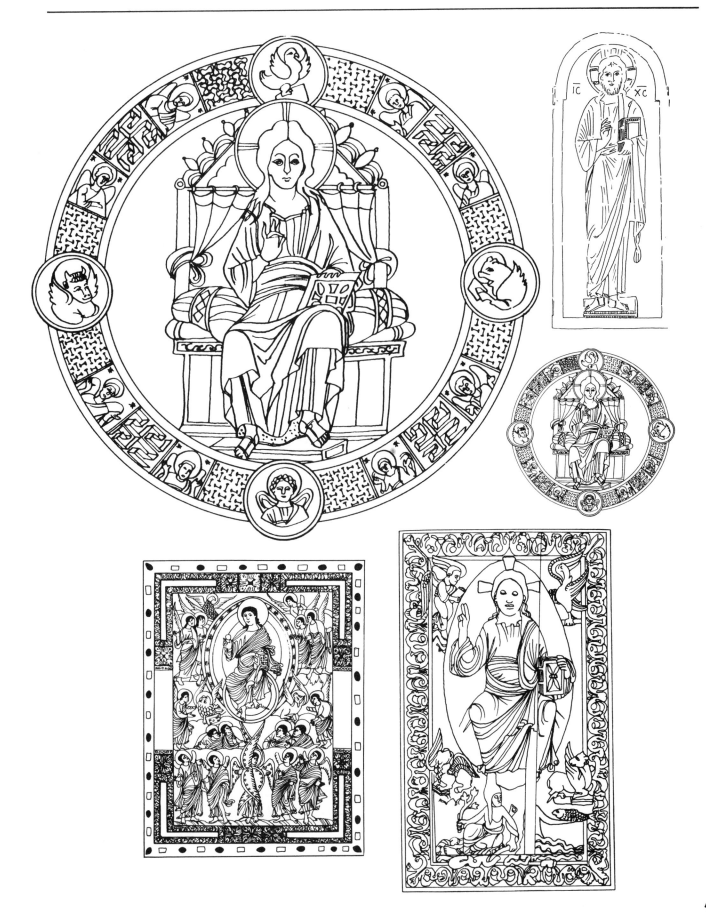

*Let
Him
easter in us,
be
a dayspring
to the
dimness of us,
be a
crimson-
cresseted
east!*

**GERARD
MANLEY HOPKINS**

*Christual
is risen
from the dead,
trampling
death
by
death,
and
to those
in the grave
bestowing
Life!
Alleluia!
Alleluia!
Alleluia!*

**ORTHODOX EASTER
TROPARION**

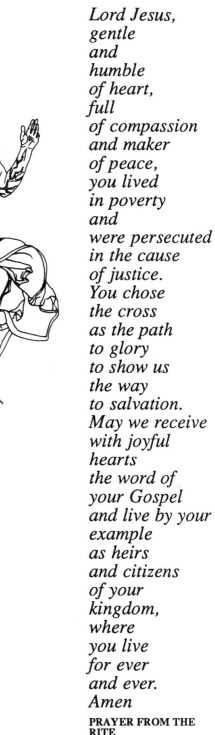

Lord Jesus,
gentle
and
humble
of heart,
full
of compassion
and maker
of peace,
you lived
in poverty
and
were persecuted
in the cause
of justice.
You chose
the cross
as the path
to glory
to show us
the way
to salvation.
May we receive
with joyful
hearts
the word of
your Gospel
and live by your
example
as heirs
and citizens
of your
kingdom,
where
you live
for ever
and ever.
Amen

**PRAYER FROM THE
RITE
OF RECONCILIATION**

*You
descended
to the grave,
Immortal One,
yet you
crushed
hell's power
and rose
a conqueror,
O Christ, God!
You spoke
a word of light
to the
myrrh-bearing
women,
"Rejoice!"
and upon
the apostles,
"Peace!"
and to the fallen
you bring
resurrection!*
ORTHODOX CHANT

He who
first said to
Adam
"Where
are you?"
is raised upon
the cross
that they
who were lost
might
be found.
And descending
to hell
Christ
proclaims:
"Come,
my Image,
my Likeness!"
ST EPHREM

ANACIACIC

*Upon
his own
he breathes
new life:
His wounds
emblazon
hands and side..
Behold in him
our Lord
and God;
the Risen One,
the Crucified.*

**THE
DAYSPRING HYMNAL**

*We sense that
there can be
no
true communion
between
human beings
until they
have in fact
become beings:
for to be able
to give oneself
one must have
taken possession
of oneself
in that painful
solitude
outside of which
nothing
belongs to us,
and we have
nothing to
give....*
LOUIS LAVELLE

INFER
DIGI
TV
M

TVVM
HVI
FIN
DE

You are apostles in the Church and in the world, in the things of the Spirit and in the things of the world.

RITE OF CONSECRATION OF WOMEN LIVING IN THE WORLD

*Now tell us,
Mary;
say
what you saw
along the way:
"The tomb
where life
once lay:
Christ in glory
ris'n
today!"*

THE EASTER SEQUENCE

*She suffers
wounds
that will not heal
and enters
into the pain
of God
where lives
the gardener
who once exalted
in her perfume,
knew
the extravagance
of her hair,
and now asks her
whom she seeks.*
JOHN SHEA

*...There
was no sound
to prepare us,
no noise of
miracle,
no trumpet
announcing
the death
of death,
-or was it
what we call
life?
We did not
understand
and we ran
from the
empty tomb
and then
he came to us
in silence.
He did not
explain
and at last
I knew
that only in
silence
is the Word.*
MADALENE L'ENGLE

71

"If I be lifted up,
I will draw all
things to myself."
-here is the open
embrace of all
humanity.
If we are to be
one with Christ
who is the
Only One,
the closer we
must be to others
who are also
trying to be
one with Christ,
for we are
only able to
talk about the
"Pleroma"
of Christ.
Therefore,
if I am open
to Christ
to become more
"me,"
I must be open
to the other
who is also
Christ.

DAMASUS WINZEN

"Why
stand then
looking
heavenward?"
Christ
dwells in us;
we, in the Lord!
Beyond both
earth
and heav'n above
our lives
are hidden
in his love.
**THE
DAYSPRING HYMNAL**

ΑΝΑΡΕCΓΑΛΙΛΑΙΟΙ
ΤΙΕCΤΗΚΑΤΕΒΛΕΠΟΝ
ΤΕCΕΙCΤΟΝΟΥΡΑΝΟΝ

*In our union
with Christ
Jesus,
God has
raised us up
with him*
EPHESIANS 2:6

From death
to Life
we have been
raised,
from earth
to heaven we are
led,
by Christ,
our
Resurrection
Joy,
for he is risen
as he said!

Let all of heaven
burst with joy!
Let all the earth
with song
resound!
Let all creation
join the dance
for Christ is
risen,
death is bound!

O Victim
indestructable;
O Saviour-God:
Love
self-effaced!
In rising
to our Abba's
throne
you raised up
Eve and Adam's
race!

**THE
DAYSPRING HYMNAL**
*verses adapted from
the Great Easter Canon
of St John Damascene*

Love of our Abba,
Love of God
the Son,
in whom
all things dwell,
in whom all is One;
raising
new wonders
even out of strife:
Spirit, dwell in us:
breathe in us
your Life!

You, the All-Holy,
wholly our delight!
Peace
is your present;
in your presence,
Light!
Earth,
cared and cradled,
lies in your
embrace:
Flame in us
your fire;
free us
in your grace!

Mother-like,
nurt'ring,
wise, sincere
and just:
Truth
ever-timeless,
source of all
our trust:
Touch
the human heart
and it is
enthralled;
ravish us, Spirit!
Come,
be All-in-All!

**THE
DAYSPRING HYMNAL**

*In
the form
of the
crucified,
humiliated
and problematic,
yet eternally
worthy
of worship,
lies a judgement
but also
a justification
for all
human attempts
at creating form.
In his triumph
lies also
the possibility
of the miracle
which we can
never attain,
but which
is given us
as grace:
the experience
of the Holy
through
the beautiful.*

**GERARDUS
VAN DER LEEUW**

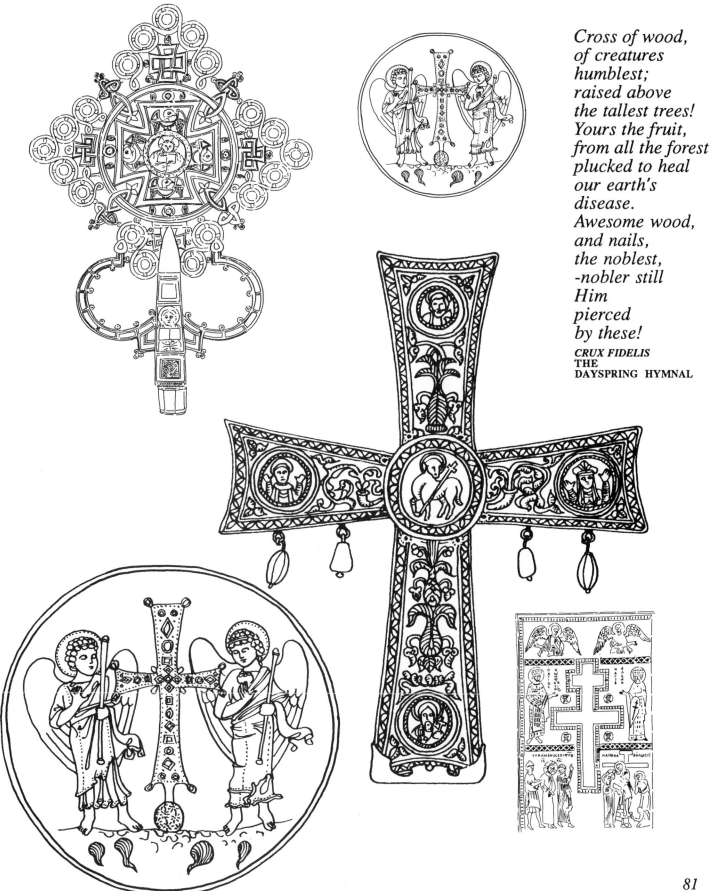

*Cross of wood,
of creatures
humblest;
raised above
the tallest trees!
Yours the fruit,
from all the forest
plucked to heal
our earth's
disease.
Awesome wood,
and nails,
the noblest,
-nobler still
Him
pierced
by these!*
CRUX FIDELIS
THE
DAYSPRING HYMNAL

We venerate
the wood
of your Cross,
O Lover
of our race,
for upon it,
You
the Life-giver
of all
were nailed.
To the thief
who turned
to you in faith,
O Saviour,
paradise
was opened
wide.
He cried out,
"O Lord
remember me,"
confessed to you,
and
you lavished him
with blessedness.
Accept us, also,
as we confess:
We have sinned,
each one of us;
in your tender
compassion
do not turn
from us.
ORTHODOX CHANT

*"Come,"
my heart
has said,
"Seek
God's face."
It is your face,
O Lord,
that I seek;
do not hide it
from me.*
PSALM 27:8

84

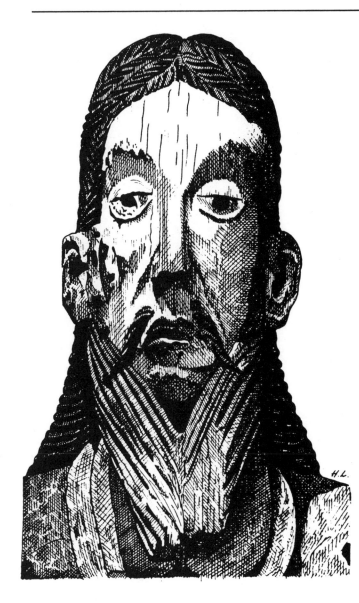

"The question is not whether someone is seeking God or not, but whether one is seeking God where God has chosen to be revealed." That locus consists of the world of the poor....

KARL RAHNER
quoted by JON SOBRINO

...*On that day
we
shall see you,
our God,
as you are.
We shall become
like you
and praise you
for ever....*

**ROMAN
EUCHARISTIC PRAYER
III**

86

The love of God
is like a fire
in our hearts
that burns
brighter
and brighter,
and the sparks
that fly out
from it
are our
smaller loves,
which belong to it
and fall back
into the fulness
of the flame.
It is a fire
that
carries us up
with it
to the supreme
goodness of God,
in which
all smaller loves
are turned into
the love of God.
Therefore
we cannot
simply say that
we love ourselves
or our neighbor,
for we love them
with a love that
is wholly
consumed
by God,
since
we are unable
to see anything
but
God's very Self.
ST AELRED OF RIEVAULX

*I saw
a storm wind
coming
from the north,
a vast cloud
with flashes
of fire
and brilliant
light
about it;
and within
was a radiance
like brass,
glowing in the
heart
of the flames.
In the fire
was the
semblance
of four living
creatures
in human form...
Their faces
were like this:
all four
had the face
of a man
and the face
of a lion
on the right,
on the left
the face
of an ox
and the face
of an eagle...*
EZEKIEL 1:4-5, 10

90

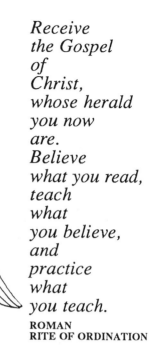

*Receive
the Gospel
of
Christ,
whose herald
you now
are.
Believe
what you read,
teach
what
you believe,
and
practice
what
you teach.*
**ROMAN
RITE OF ORDINATION**

*In the center,
round
the throne itself,
were four
living creatures,
covered
with eyes,
in front and
behind.
The first
creature
was like a lion,
the second like
an ox,
the third
had a
human face,
the fourth
was like
an eagle
in flight...*

REVELATION 4:7-8

*The very
existence
of the Bible
understood
as a normative
collection
of books
supposes
an ongoing
community
willing
to shape itself
by responding
to that
norm.*

RAYMOND BROWN

ASACERDOTU·LUCASTENET·ORA·IUBENCI

When you
come
into contact
with
some share of
Scripture's
treasure,
do not think
that
the only thing
contained
in the word
is what
you, yourself,
have found.
Realize
that you
have only
been able
to find
that one thing
from
among many
others.
Nor, because
only that
one part has
become yours,
should you say
the word is
void and empty
and so look
down on it;
rather,
because you
could not
exhaust it,
give thanks
for its riches.
ST EPHREM

*Today
we honor
John,
the
virgin apostle
who
drank the
Gospel-streams
from
their very source,
the Lord's own
breast.
How great
his happiness,
to whom
heaven's
mysteries
were
all revealed!
Alleluia*

**BENEDICTUS ANTIPHON:
FEAST OF ST JOHN**
MONASTIC RITE

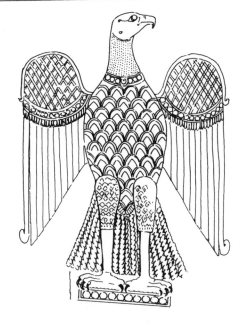

I think
I understand
why the psalmist
calls God
a "friendly" God,
namely, because
God tolerates us
with all our
faults and
failures,
at the same time
expecting us
to pray
so that
in God
we might
be matured.
And when
we make
our prayer
before God,
God accepts it
willingly
and grants
our petitions,
not remembering
our many
distractions
but welcoming
the one prayer
which we
succeeded in
praying
in quiet and
peace.
ST AUGUSTINE

*If God speaks
to us,
it is certainly
not to "chat"
with us
about
something
or other.
God's word
always aims
at the
very existence
of the one
to whom it is
addressed.
"For God spoke,
and it was done"
(Psalm 33:9)
The new word
that God
addresses to us
must be
a new creation,
a "word of Life,"
opening us
to a new
dimension.
It was the
fall of humanity
which gave
God
the opportunity
to speak a new
word,
the word
of mercy
and forgiveness.*
DAMASUS WINZEN

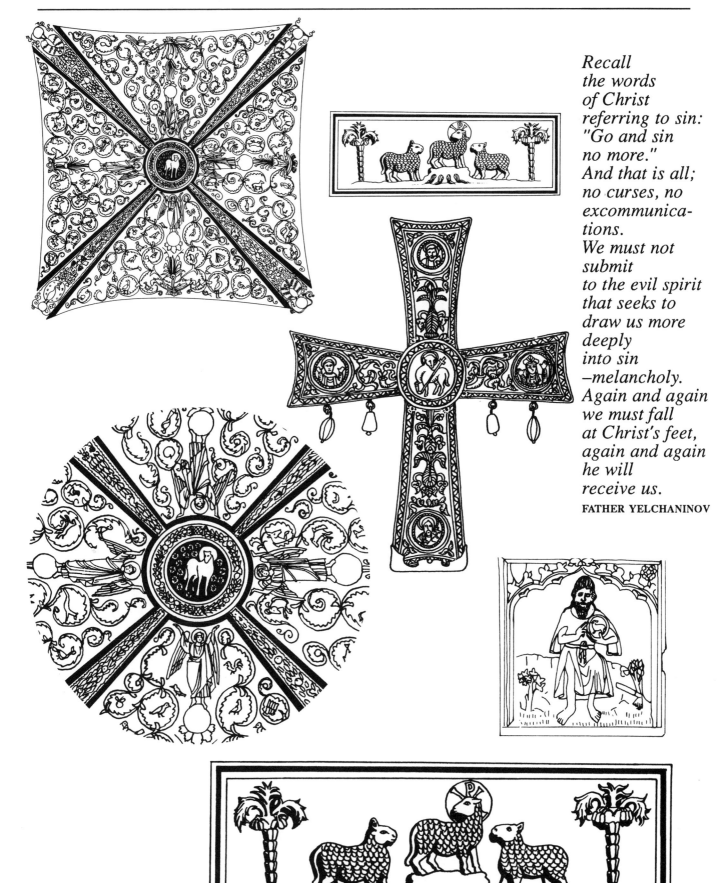

Recall
the words
of Christ
referring to sin:
"Go and sin
no more."
And that is all;
no curses, no
excommunica-
tions.
We must not
submit
to the evil spirit
that seeks to
draw us more
deeply
into sin
—melancholy.
Again and again
we must fall
at Christ's feet,
again and again
he will
receive us.

FATHER YELCHANINOV

*It is love itself,
by
its very
presence
that
pronounces
judgement.*
LOUIS BOUYER

*Bring us,
O Lord God,
at our last
awakening
into the house
and gate of
heaven,
to enter into that
gate
and dwell in that
house,
where there
shall be
no darkness
nor dazzling,
but one equal
light;
no noise nor
silence,
but one equal
music;
no fears nor
hopes,
but one
equal possession;
no ends nor
beginnings,
but one equal
eternity;
in the
habitations
of thy glory
and
dominion
world
without
end.*
JOHN DONNE

*I am
espoused
to Him
whom
the angels
serve;
sun and moon
stand
in wonder
at
his glory.*
**ANTIPHON:
CONSECRATION
OF A VIRGIN**

*My
soul
glorifies
the Lord:
my
spirit
rejoices
in
God
my Saviour,
who
has looked
on me
in my
emptiness.*
MARY'S SONG

Hail,
raft for all
struggling to be
saved!
Hail,
haven
to swimmers
upon the world's
waves!
BYZANTINE
AKATHIST HYMN

*I have been deaf
and deaf
to the pulse
of the heartbeat
of
the dumb women
who carry
the seed of
the world's wheat.
Because my
neighbor's need
has been simple
and like my own,
Christ,
the close friend
of the hearth,
the known,
has been
unknown.*
CARYLL HOUSELANDER

God,
invulnerable,
asked her
for tears.
God, truly God,
asked
to be born
her son.
God asked her
for hands
and feet to be
nailed.
God asked her
for flesh
to be scourged.
God asked her
for blood
to be shed.
God asked her
for a heart
to be broken.
**adapted from
CARYLL HOUSELANDER**

...mind
without soul
may blast some
universe
to
might have been
and stop
ten thousand stars
but
not one heartbeat
of this child;
nor shall even
prevail
a million
questionings
against
the silence
of his mother's
smile
—whose
only secret
all creation sings

e. e. cummings

*Virgin
of deep
star-night
stillness;
Virgin
of archangel-
bright
brilliance;
Earthen-vessel,
Heaven-bearing;
Thou, the Dawn
of Christ's
appearing!
Woman
in the fullest
measure;
fallow field
of hidden
treasure;
Mary,
we pray thee,
be mother—
shelter us
in thy Son,
Jesus, our
brother.*

AVE REGINA CAELORUM
THE
DAYSPRING HYMNAL

*Birth-Giver
of God,
you are graced!
ALLELUIA
For Christ
the Fruit
of your womb
has been raised!
ALLELUIA
He is risen
and we with him!
ALLELUIA
Your blest
consent
has done this!
ALLELUIA*
**REGINA COELI
DAYSPRING HYMNAL**

*God-bearing
Mother,
whence sprung
the Father's
tender love!
Light
to our darkness!
Hope,
the world
despairs of!
With night's
unfolding,
gathered
once again
in Christ-love,
our hearts
take up their rest;
our longings and
our fears
confidently
we take leave of—
Peace-filled
we pray:
You who shared
your son's cross:
take to yourself
the suff'rings
Christ
must still endure
—the sword
once spoken of—
Our Blessing
be in the
blessedness
of your hallowed
womb: Jesus,
in whom
we are newborn
to life above.
O Loving mother!
O Tender One!
O Gentle One!
Virgin Mary!*

**A NEW "SALVE"
DAYSPRING HYMNAL**

Rejoice,
rejoice,
daughter
of Zion,
shout aloud,
daughter
of Jerusalem;
for see,
your king
is coming
to you,
his cause
won,
his victory
gained!
ZECHARIAH 9:9

*Blessed
is he
who
comes in the
name
of the Lord!
Hosanna
in the highest!*
THE SANCTUS
(PSALM 118: 26)

*In performing
your ministry
bear in mind
that,
as you share
the one bread
with your
brothers
and sisters,
so you form
one body
with them.
Show a sincere
love for
Christ's
Mystical Body,
God's
holy people,
and especially
for the weak
and the sick.
Be obedient
to the
commandment
which
the Lord gave
to his apostles
at the
Last Supper:
"Love
one another
as I also
have loved you."*

**RITE OF INSTITUTION
OF ACOLYTES**

*Accept from
the holy people
of God
the gifts
to be offered to
God.
Know
what you do
and imitate
the mystery
you celebrate;
model your life
on the mystery of
the Lord's cross.*
**ROMAN
RITE OF ORDINATION**

*Holy Gifts
for
a Holy People!
Only
One is holy!
Only One
is Lord!
Jesus Christ,
to the Glory
of the
Father!*
**LITURGY
OF
ST JOHN CHRYSOSTOM**

ÓΝΙΠΤΗΡ

ÓΝΙΠΤΗΡ

Where
compassion,
care and love
abound,
there
our God is found!

We are gathered
here together,
bound by
Christ's love,
and this love
overwhelms us,
fills us,
floods us with joy!

In one Body
we have all
been gathered:
One, now, in
Christ!
There is neither
male or female;
divisions cease!

Let each of us
with unveiled
faces
behold God's
Face;
and behold in
one another's
features
Christ manifest!

Then boundless
will be the joy
we bear,
the happiness,
both here
and in the fulness
of the Kingdom,
for ages unending.
Amen

UBI CARITAS
THE
DAYSPRING HYMNAL

*L*ET
us therefore be of one mind,
one heart,
one voice,
and in the midst of our gath'ring here
let Christ-God
be All in All!

*Suffering
does not
diminish us,
but reveals us
to ourselves....
There are
thresholds
that thought,
left to its
own resources,
can never cross;
an experience
is needed-
poverty,
sickness....
It is as if
our eyes are
opened
and we can see
things
that we never
even dreamed.
Perhaps
the world, itself,
is given another
dimension.*
GABRIEL MARCEL

*While
you prayed
the earth
blossomed,
and see,
all
is ripe
for the
harvest....*
PAUL CLAUDEL

*Thirty years
Christ
lived our brother,
servant
to the
very end.
This his path,
he sought
no other;
to his passion
gave consent:
crucified
before
his mother:
hung
condemned,
though
innocent.*
**THE
DAYSPRING HYMNAL**

*In the practice
of justice the
transcendence
of God
manifests itself
in a different
and more
radical way.
The mystery
of the ever
greater God
seems to be
mediated
through
the"more"
attached to the
obligation
to humanize
and recreate
human beings.*
JON SOBRINO

127

*I have come
to suspect
that a part of
God's silence
is my own;
that a part
of God's
absence is
nothing
but the
absence of
our own
hearts,
of our
humanity,
of our
friendships-
I would not
venture
to say
our love,
for we are not
capable
of love.
The absences
of the
human heart
last
a long time.
Then who
are we
to judge God?*

PETRU DUMITRIU

*Christ
became
for us
obedient
unto death,
even
the death
of the
Cross.
And therefore
God
has highly
exalted him:
and
given him
a name
which
is above
every name!*

**RESPONSORY:
GOOD FRIDAY**
(Philippians 2:9-11)

*Lord Jesus,
from
your wounded
side
flowed
streams
of cleansing
water:
the world
was washed
of all its sin;
all life
made new
again!*
**RITE
OF CHRISTIAN
INITIATION**

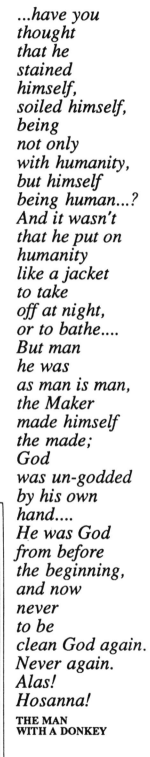

...have you
thought
that he
stained
himself,
soiled himself,
being
not only
with humanity,
but himself
being human...?
And it wasn't
that he put on
humanity
like a jacket
to take
off at night,
or to bathe....
But man
he was
as man is man,
the Maker
made himself
the made;
God
was un-godded
by his own
hand....
He was God
from before
the beginning,
and now
never
to be
clean God again.
Never again.
Alas!
Hosanna!

**THE MAN
WITH A DONKEY**

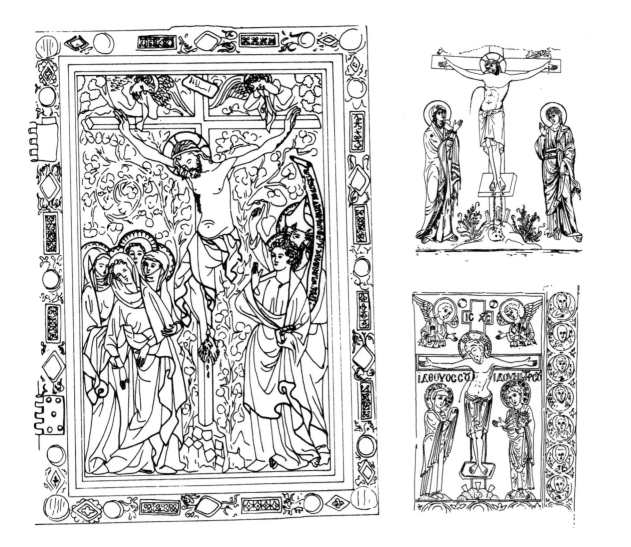

*O God,
you were pleased
to hallow
the standard
of the
life-giving Cross
with the
precious blood
of your
only-begotten
Son;
we pray you,
grant
that those
who delight
in honoring
this holy Cross
may everywhere
rejoice
in your
protection.*

**VOTIVE MASS
OF THE HOLY CROSS**
MISSAL OF PIUS V

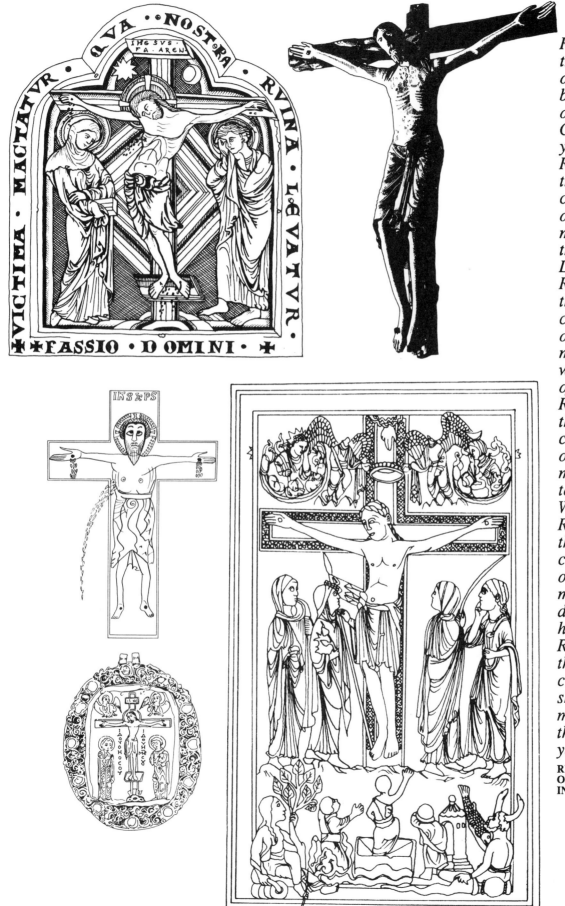

*Receive
the cross
on your forehead:
by this sign
of his triumph
Christ will be
your strength.
Receive
the sign of the
cross
on your ears:
may you hear
the voice of the
Lord.
Receive
the sign of the
cross
on your eyes:
may you see
with the light
of God.
Receive
the sign of the
cross
on your lips:
may you respond
to the
Word of God.
Receive
the sign of the
cross
on your breast:
may Christ
dwell in your
heart by faith.
Receive
the sign of the
cross on your
shoulders:
may you accept
the sweet
yoke of Christ.*

**RITE
OF CHRISTIAN
INITIATION**

136

Jesus Christ is always on the side of the crucified, and I believe he changes sides in the twinkling of an eye. He is not loyal to the person, or even less to the group; he is loyal to suffering.
PETRU DUMITRIU

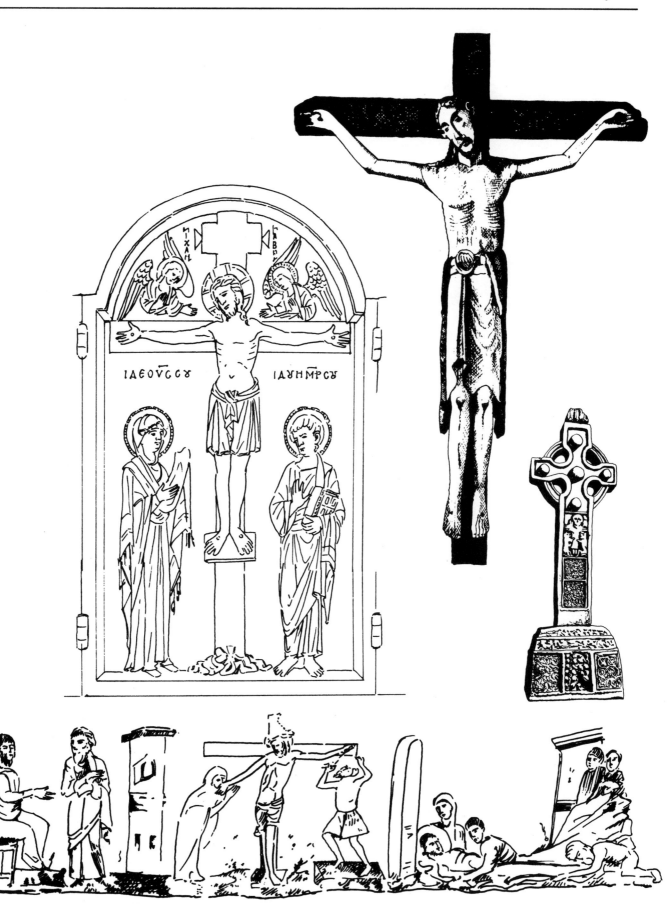

*Let us
glory
in the cross
of our Lord
Jesus Christ,
in whom is
our salvation,
our life
& resurrection;
in whom
we have been
saved
and set free!*

**EXALTATION OF
THE HOLY CROSS
(GAL. 6:14)**

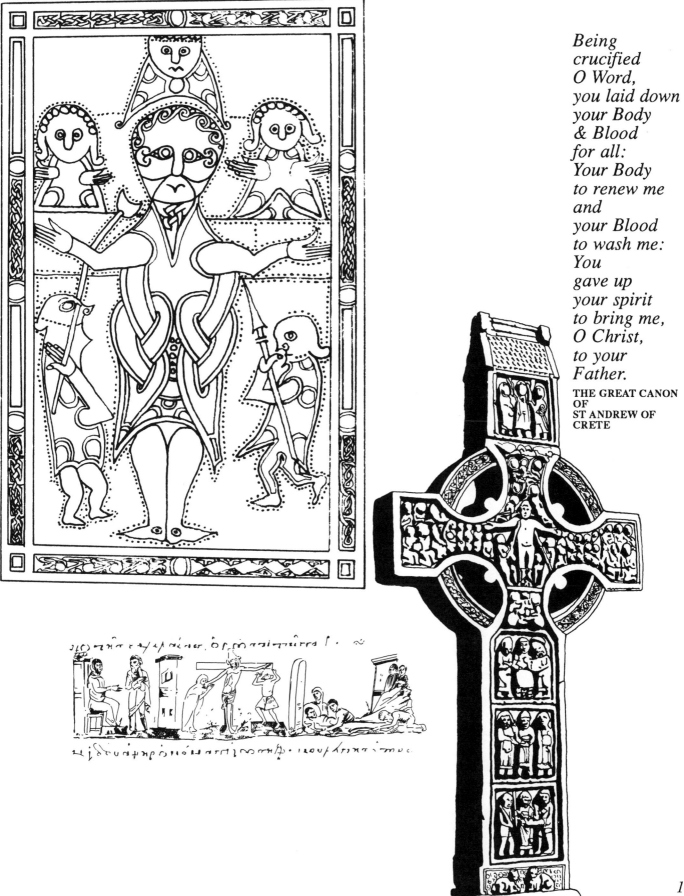

Being
crucified
O Word,
you laid down
your Body
& Blood
for all:
Your Body
to renew me
and
your Blood
to wash me:
You
gave up
your spirit
to bring me,
O Christ,
to your
Father.

**THE GREAT CANON
OF
ST ANDREW OF
CRETE**

141

*We
adore you
O Christ,
and we bless
you,
because
by your Cross
you have
redeemed
the
whole world.*
CHANT OF GOOD FRIDAY

Immortal,
Holy,
Mighty God,
whose love for us
by spear
springs forth!
We
bow before this
Mystery:
Life
self-consumed
in holocaust!

THE
DAYSPRING HYMNAL

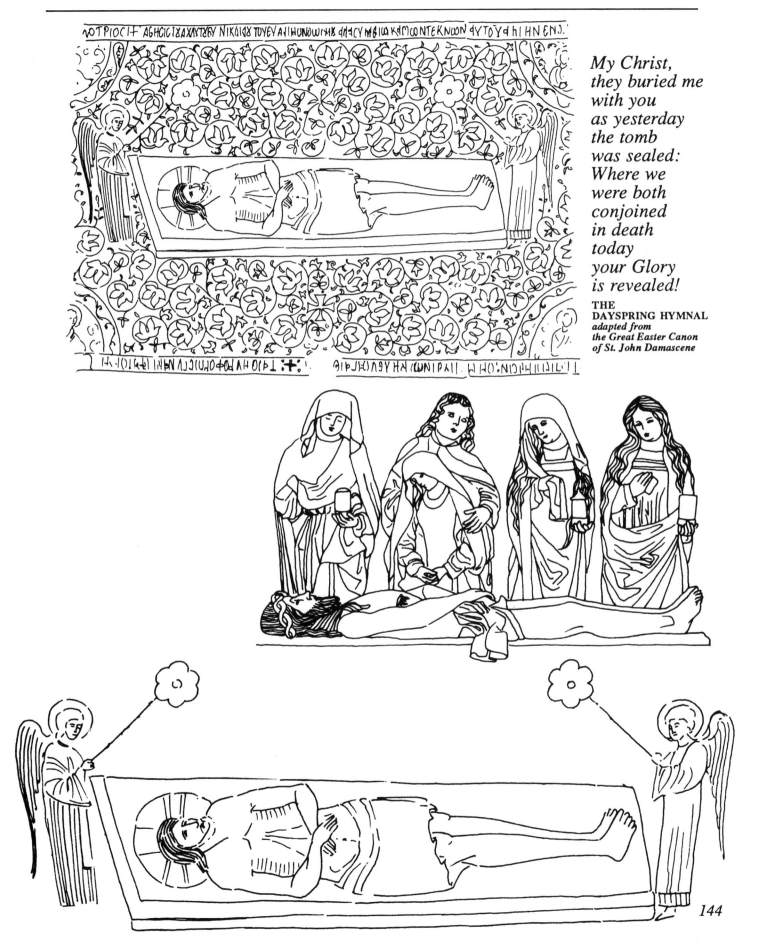

My Christ,
they buried me
with you
as yesterday
the tomb
was sealed:
Where we
were both
conjoined
in death
today
your Glory
is revealed!

**THE
DAYSPRING HYMNAL**
*adapted from
the Great Easter Canon
of St. John Damascene*

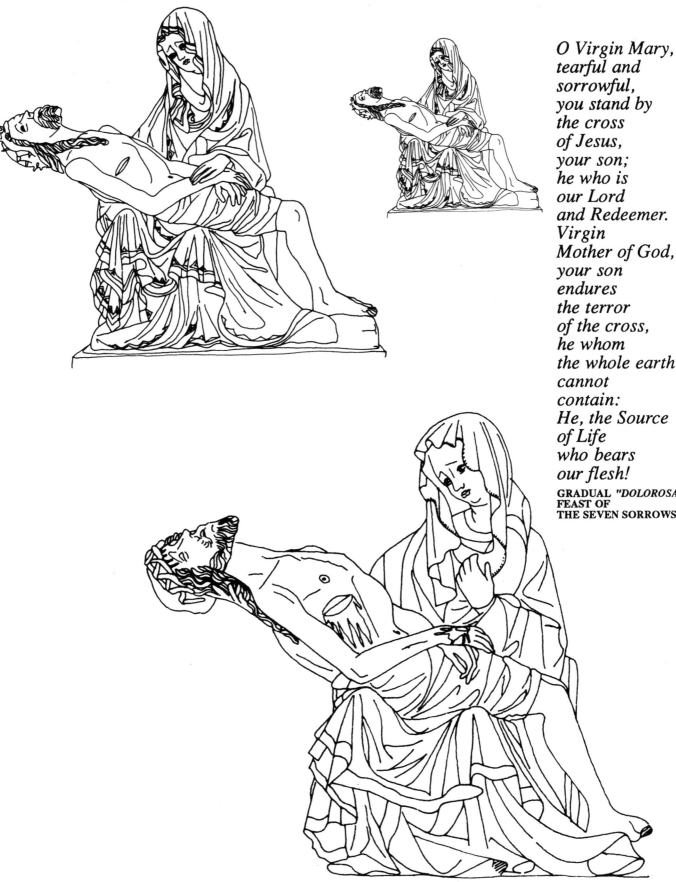

*O Virgin Mary,
tearful and
sorrowful,
you stand by
the cross
of Jesus,
your son;
he who is
our Lord
and Redeemer.
Virgin
Mother of God,
your son
endures
the terror
of the cross,
he whom
the whole earth
cannot
contain:
He, the Source
of Life
who bears
our flesh!*

**GRADUAL "DOLOROSA:"
FEAST OF
THE SEVEN SORROWS**

*Where
indeed
should your
Light
have shown
except
upon
those
who sit
in darkness?*
ORTHODOX CHANT

*Today
he who
suspended
earth above
the waters
is suspended
now
upon the Cross.
He, the king
of angels
is crowned
with thorns.
He who clothes
with clouds
the heavens,
is cloaked
with purple
mockery.
He, who
in the Jordan
set Eve & Adam
free,
is set upon with
blows.
The Bridegroom
of the Church
is bound with
nails.
The Son of the
Virgin
is pierced now
with a spear.*
**ORTHODOX CHANT
FOR GOOD FRIDAY**

*...Let us think
of the sufferings of
God within us,
and of all
the atrocious
sufferings
taking place
at this
very moment,
in God.
Let us think of
those
who think of us
without
knowing us,
let us think of
those who pray,
of all the silent
multitude of souls
at prayer.
We are not alone.
In solitude,
silence,
forsakeness,
in the sleep of
matter,
the sound and fury
of suffering,
of birth,
of coupling,
of despair,
of evil and good,
there is every-
where the peace
of prayer,
everywhere
glimmers of grace.
There is the
church of souls.*

PETRU DUMITRIU

*The old man
held the child
in his arms,
but
the child
held sovereignty
over
his elder.
The Virgin
who had borne
the child,
remained
a virgin
after
giving birth,
adoring
as her God
the child
she had borne.*

**MAGNIFICAT ANTIPHON
OF THE FEAST**

*Sion,
prepare your
bridal chamber
to receive
Christ your
King:
Lovingly
welcome
Mary,
Gate of Heaven,
for she it is
who brings you
the King
of Light & Glory.
Behold
the Virgin,
holding
in her arms
the Son
begotten
before the
morning star:
Simeon,
taking him
into his arms,
proclaims
to all the nations
this is
the Lord
of life and death,
the Saviour
of the World.*

**OLD ANTIPHON
OF THE FEAST**

*Let us all
go to meet Christ
with eager hearts:
Let there
be none
who do not
share in
this encounter;
let no one
refuse
to carry a light...
In this way
we show forth
the divine
splendor
of his coming,
who makes
all things bright,
in the brilliance
of whose
eternal light
all is bathed
in light....*
ST SOPHRONIUS

*Do not think
that saintliness
comes from
occupation.
It depends,
rather,
on what one is.
The kind of work
we do does not
make us holy
but we may
make it holy.
Hovever
"sacred"
a calling may be,
as it is
a "calling"
it has no power
to sanctify:
but rather
as we are
and have the
Divine Being
within us,
we bless each
task we do,
be it eating,
or sleeping,
or watching,
or any other.
—Thus take care
that your
emphasis
is on being good
and not on the
number
or kind of things
to be done.
Emphasize
rather
the fundamentals
on which
your work
depends.*

MEISTER ECKHART

152

✝ SC S STHEFA NVS

✝ SC S STHEFA NVS

*—Christ plays
in ten thousand
places,
Lovely in limbs,
and lovely
in eyes not his
To the Father
through the
features
of men's faces.*
**GERARD
MANLEY HOPKINS**

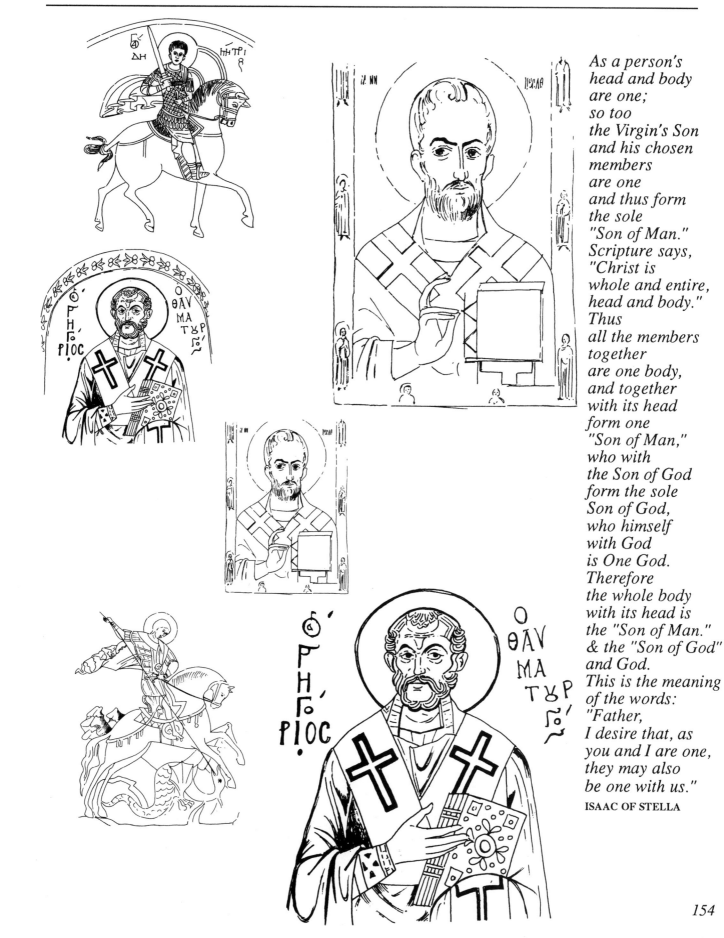

As a person's
head and body
are one;
so too
the Virgin's Son
and his chosen
members
are one
and thus form
the sole
"Son of Man."
Scripture says,
"Christ is
whole and entire,
head and body."
Thus
all the members
together
are one body,
and together
with its head
form one
"Son of Man,"
who with
the Son of God
form the sole
Son of God,
who himself
with God
is One God.
Therefore
the whole body
with its head is
the "Son of Man."
& the "Son of God"
and God.
This is the meaning
of the words:
"Father,
I desire that, as
you and I are one,
they may also
be one with us."

ISAAC OF STELLA

*The ways
of the Lord
are thus:
To begin with,
God seeks us,
God's face
is revealed
to us,
and we are
drawn
to God's eternity.
Then God
may return us
to the framework
of time.
There
would seem
to be no sense
to this return
other than
to entrust us
with manifesting
in our life
the knowledge
given us
of the I AM,
and to bear
witness
to God's love
for us....*
STARETZ SILOUAN

155

*This day
on the
holy mountain
Christ
showed
his chosen
disciples,
our created
nature
clothed
in God's
immortal Image!*
ORTHODOX CHANT

156

*Transfigured
on
Mount Tabor's
height
a new creation
was unveiled;
yet You, alone,
could show us
what
this path to
Glory
would entail—*
**THE
DAYSPRING HYMNAL**

The Lord
appeared
to Abraham
by the oaks
of Mamre.
As Abraham
was sitting
at the opening
of his tent
in the heat
of the day,
he looked up
and saw
three travelers
standing in front
of him.
When he saw
them,
he ran from his
tent
to meet them
and bowed low
to the ground.

GENESIS 18:1-2

*God
making
all that is
before our day:
God guiding all
that's made
throughout our
day:
Gift that abides
through
an eternity
of giving,
yet made no less.
Your going-forth
preceded time,
your pouring-
forth
took place in
time.
The one,
the well-spring
of power
and
the river
of grace,
the other,
the flowing,
the giving,
the light
on our face...*

HILDEBERT (1056-1133)
trans. Helen Waddell

159

...to our cry
of distress
God could cry:
"Why have
you forsaken
each other?
I granted you
forgetfulness
of suffering,
and
forgetfulness
of offences:
why do you
use this gift
to forget your
sins?
Is it just so
you need not
repent,
that you need not
learn
from your
experiences,
and never repeat
them?

PETRU DUMITRIU

SOURCES

ANNUNCIATION

7   Diptych of Bishop Grandison (ivory), mid-14th c., British Museum, London.
    Icon, known as the Virgin of Ustiug, 1119-30, Tretyakov Gallery, Moscow.
    St. Albans Psalter, 1125, St.Godehard Treasury, Hildesheim, Germany.
    Icon, 14th c., Nat. Mus., Skopje, Yugoslavia.
8   Gospels of S. Martin-le-Grand, Cologne, 13th c., Bibl. Roy., Brussels.
    Icon, known as the Virgin of Ustiug, 1119-30, Tretyakov Gallery, Moscow.
    Diptych of Bishop Grandison (ivory), mid-14th c., British Museum, London.
    St. Albans Psalter, 1125, St. Godehard Treasury, Hildesheim, Germany.

APOSTLES: Peter

9   Bas-relief on portal, 1110-20, Abbey Church of S. Pierre, Moissac, France.
    Icon, c. 600, Monastery of St Catherine, Mount Sinai.
    Portal figure, late 12th c., Cathedral of S. Trophime, Arles, France.

APOSTLES: Paul

10 Wood, c.1500, Archiepiscopal Museum, Utrecht, Netherlands.
    Mosaic, 1140-54, Cappella Palatina, Palermo, Sicily.
    Stone, by Nino Pisano,1363, Cathedral Mus., Pisa, Italy.

APOSTLES: John, James, Philip

11 James the Greater, 1165-75, Capilla S. Miguel, Cathedral, Oviedo, Spain.
    James (?), after 1117, Portico de los Orfebres, Cathedral of St James, Santiago de Compostella, Spain.
    John, 1165-75, Capilla S. Miguel, Cathedral, Oviedo, Spain.
    Philip (capital), late 7th c., San Pedro de la Nave, Spain.

APOSTLES: Others

12 Apostle (ambulatory plaque), late 11th c., Church of St Sernin, Toulouse, France.
    Apostle (stained glass panel), c.1330-40, Schloss Friedrichshafen, Germany.
    Apostle (stone figure on façade), 1220-35, Amiens Cathedral, France.
    Apostle (reliquary plaque), 1059, Treasury of the Church of St Isidoro, León, Spain.
    Detail, Box reliquary of the Holy Cross (lid/enamel), c. 960, Limburg Cathedral Treasury, Germany.

ASSUMPTION/DORMITION OF THE VIRGIN

13 Enamel triptych, 10th-11th c., Bayerische St. Mus., Munich.
    Ivory book cover, c. 900, Abbey Library, St Gall, Switzerland.
    Wall painting, 14th c., Church of St Peter, Berende, Bulgaria.
14 Ivory book cover, c. 900, Abbey Library, St Gall, Switzerland.
    Icon, 15th c., Monastery of St John the Evangelist, Patmos, Greece.
    Wall painting, 14th c., Church of St Peter, Berende, Bulgaria.

CHI RHO

15 Ravenna-style sarcophagus, 6th c., S. Apollinare in Classe, Ravenna.
    Roman sarcophagus, c. 400, S. Rocco, Frascati, Italy.
    Silver paten from Malaya Pereshepina, U.S.S.R., 491-518, Hermitage, Leningrad.
    Child's sarcophagus, c. 400, Archaeol. Mus., Istanbul.

CHRIST AND APOSTLES

16 Gates of the city on Christian sarcophagus, c. 390, Basilica of S. Ambrogio, Milan, Italy.
    Christ and St John (stone), c.1330, St. Mus., Berlin/Dahlem, Germany.
    Christ in majesty and the apostles (altar frontal), 11th-12th c., Mus. de Arte de Cataluña, Barcelona.
17 Christ in majesty and the apostles (altar frontal), 11th-12th c., Mus. de Arte de Cataluña, Barcelona.
    Christ in majesty and the apostles (lintel, or retablo), 1020-21, Saint-Genis-des-Fontaines, France.

CHRISTMAS CYCLE: Nativity
18 Miniature, 15th c., Church at Queddus Gabre'el, Lake Tana, Ethiopia.
    Wooden retablo from the Middle Rhine, mid-14th c., private coll.
    Ivory plaque on Chair of Maximian, mid-6th c., Archiepiscopal Mus., Ravenna, Italy.
    Polychrome wood, by Adriaen van Wesel, 14700-80, Rijksmus., Amsterdam.
19 (Detail) Five-part book cover of the Lorsch Gospels, c.800, Victoria and Albert Mus., London.
    Mosaic, 1143-51, Martorana, Palermo, Sicily.
    Detail (sheep), wall painting of the Burning Bush, c. 1321, Church of the Annunciation, Gracanica, Yugoslavia.
20 Detail, triptych, 10-11th cen., Louvre, Paris.
    Wood engraving from Upper Rhine, c.1420, Bibliothèque Nat., Paris.
    Capital, late 12th c., Cathedral of S. Sauveur, Aix-en-Provence, France.
    Bust of the sun in a medallion (stone relief), c.700, Santa Maria de Quintanilla, Spain.
21 Wooden retablo from the Middle Rhine, mid-14th c., private coll.
    Miniature, 15th c., Church at Queddus Gabre'el, Lake Tana, Ethiopia.

CHRISTMAS CYCLE: Adoration of the Magi
22 Ampulla, late 6th c., Tesorio della Basilica, Monza, Italy.
    Detail of fresco, late 12th c., Church of St Martin, Vicq, France.
23 Miniature, Ingeborg Psalter, c.1200, Mus. Condé, Chantilly, France.
    Ampulla, late 6th c., Tesorio della Basilica, Monza, Italy.
    Detail of fresco, late 12th c., Church of St Martin, Vicq, France.
    The Franks Casket (Northumbrian morse ivory), c. 700, British Museum, London.
24 Miniature, Ingeborg Psalter, c.1200, Mus. Condé, Chantilly, France.
25 Central portion of five-part diptych, mid-6th c., British Museum, London.
    Crozier from Angers (?), mid-12th c., Victoria and Albert Museum, London.

CHRISTMAS CYCLE: Baptism of the Lord
26 Miniature, Gospel-book No. 6201, 1038, Matenadaran, Yerevan, Armenia, U.S.S.R.
    Mosiac in dome of Arian Baptistery, c. 500, Ravenna, Italy.
27 Mosiac in dome of Arian Baptistery, c. 500, Ravenna, Italy.
28 Miniature, Gospel-book No. 6201, 1038, Matenadaran, Yerevan, Armenia, U.S.S.R.
    Icon, 14th c., Greek Patriarchate, Jerusalem.
    Baptismal font attributed to Renier de Huy (brass), 1107-18, S. Barthélémy, Liège, Belgium.

CHRISTMAS CYCLE: Wedding at Cana
29 Wall painting, 1320-40, S. Nicholas Orphanos, Salonica, Greece.

CHRISTMAS CYCLE: Flight Into Egypt
30 Tempera on wood, by Master Bertram, 1379, Kunsthalle, Hamburg, Germany.
    Nave capital, early 12th c., Cathedral of St Lazare, Autun, France.
    Mosaic, c.1320, Kahrié Cami, Istanbul.
31 Tempera on wood, by Master Bertram, 1379, Kunsthalle, Hamburg, Germany.
    Wall painting, c. 700 (?), Castelseprio, Lombardy, Italy.
    Nave capital, early 12th c., Cathedral of St Lazare, Autun, France
    Mosaic, c. 1320, Kahrié Cami, Istanbul.

CHURCHES & FURNISHINGS: Chalices
32 Tassilo chalice, possibly from Northumbria, c. 770, Abbey Treasury, Kremsmünster, Germany.
    Chalice of St. Lebuinus (ivory), early 9th c., Archiepiscopal Mus., Utrecht, Netherlands.
    Silver chalice from Syria, c. 550, British Museum, London.
    Ardagh chalice, 8th c., Nat. Mus., Dublin.
    Silver and cloisonné enamel, 10th c., St Mark's Treasury, Venice.
33 Tassilo chalice, possibly from Northumbria, c.770, Abbey Treasury, Kremsmünster, Germany.
    Copper gilt, early 14th c., Spitzer Coll., Florence, Italy.
    Chalice of Manuel Cantacuzene (jasper and silver), n.d., Monastery of Vatopédi, Mount Athos, Greece.

Ardagh chalice, 8th c., Nat. Mus., Dublin.
Chalice from Wilten Abbey, 1160-70, Kunsthistorisches Mus., Vienna.
Silver chalice from Syria, c. 550, British Museum, London.

CHURCHES & FURNISHINGS: Cloisters
34   Abbey cloisters, 12th c., Montmajour, France.
     Abbey cloisters, 1100, Moissac, France.
     Abbey cloisters, early 12th c., Silos, Spain.
     Cathedral cloisters, 12th c., Saint-Lizier, France.
     Cathedral cloisters, 1126-69 (?), Bonn, Germany.

CHURCHES & FURNISHINGS: Churches
35   Church of St Euphrosyne, 1159, Polotsk, U.S.S.R.
     Basilica of S. Zeno Maggiore, 1130-40, Campanile, early 11th c., Verona, Italy.
     Façade of Cathedral, 1230 onwards, Reims, France.
     Church of St Martin, mid-11th c., Chapaise, France.
     Panagia Chalkeon (Church of the Virgin of the Coppersmiths), 1028, Salonica, Greece.
     Cathedral, late 11th c., Pisa, Italy.
     West front of St Elisabeth, 1235 onwards, Marburg, Germany.
     Monastery of Elecki, 12th c., Chernigov, U.S.S.R.
     Cathedral of the Dormition, 12th c., Vladimir, U.S.S.R.
36   Abbey Church of St Maria, early 11th c., Campanile, 1036, Pomposa, Italy.
     Abbey church, completed c. 1200, Maria-Laach, Germany.
     Church of St Pierre, 1130-60, Aulnay, France.
     Cathedral, 1099-1184, Modena, Italy.
37   Abbey church, 1049, Ottmarsheim, France.
     Façade of Cathedral, 1230 onwards, Reims, France.
     Church of St Miniato, 12th c., Florence, Italy.
38   Cathedral, 1120-30, Mainz, Germany
     Cathedral of the Dormition, 12th c., Vladimir, U.S.S.R.
     Church (mudéjar style), late 12th c., S. Pedro de las Dueñas, Spain.
     Church of the Holy Sepulchre, c.1101, Cambridge, England.
39   Abbey Church of the Trinity, after 1062, Towers, 18th c., Caen, France.
     Basilica of S. Zeno Maggiore, 1130-40, Campanile, early 11th c., Verona, Italy.
     Church of the Holy Sepulchre, c.1101, Cambridge, England.
     Church of St Martin, mid-11th c., Chapaise, France.
     Church of the Virgin, c.1080, Apollonia, Albania.
     Cathedral, after 1130, Parma, Italy.
     Church of St Tomaso in Limine, mid-12th c., Almenno, Italy.

CHURCHES & FURNISHINGS: Reliquaries & Pyxs
40   Reliquary in the shape of a tower, Cologne, late 12th c., Hessisches Landesmus., Darmstadt, Germany.
     Pyx from Limoges (enamelled copper), 13th c., Louvre, Paris.
     Offertory box (metal), 15th c., Louvre, Paris.
     Ravenna-style sarcophagus, 6th c., S. Apollinare in Classe, Ravenna, Italy.
     Reliquary from Hochelten, Cologne, c. 1180, Victoria and Albert Museum, London.
     Reliquary of Warnebartus, Soissons, late 7th c., Stiftschatz, Beromünster, Germany.
41   Pyx from Limoges (enamelled copper), 13th c., Louvre, Paris.
     Sarcophagus from Aquitaine, mid-6th c. (?), S. Seurin, Bordeaux, France.
     Reliquary from Hochelten, Cologne, c. 1180, Victoria and Albert Museum, London.
     Ivory reliquary altar, after 750, St Ludgerus, Essen-Werden, Germany.
     Reliquary of Warnebartus, Soissons, late 7th c., Stiftschatz, Beromünster, Germany.

CHURCHES & FURNISHINGS: Windows & Doors
42 Abbey Church of St Léger, west front, 1134-55, Murbach, France.
    Door with iron fittings, south Germany.
    Georgian window, c. 650, Tbilisi, U.S.S.R.
    Double doors with iron fittings, 15th cen., south Germany.
    S. Salvador, 893, Valdedios, Spain.
    Church of St Pierre, c.1130-60, Aulnay, France.
    Church of St Abbondio, 1013-95, Como, Italy.
43 Window grille, wrought iron, 15th cen., S. Germany, Kunstgewebe Mus., Hamburg.
    Rose window, transcept, early 13th c., Chartres, France.
    Abbey Church of St Léger, west front, 1134-55, Murbach, France.
    Rose window, c.1320, Magdeburg, Germany.
    S. Salvador, 893, Valdedios, Spain.

CHURCHES & FURNISHINGS: Fonts
44 Three Marys at the tomb, 12th c., Calmenares, Spain.
    12th c., Toftrees, England.
    12th c., Cojóbar, Spain.
    Late 11th c., Montdidier, France.

CHURCHES & FURNISHINGS: Chairs
45 Bishop's throne (white marble), late 12th c., Notre-Dame-des-Doms, Avignon, France.
    Folding chair, Italian, 16th c., formerly Fulgence Coll.
    Bishop's throne (marble), consecrated 1038, Gerona, Spain.

CHURCHES & FURNISHINGS: Altars
46 Chapelle S. Michel (stone), 12th c., Bessuejouls, France.
    Christ in majesty and apostles (stone), c.1166, Avenas, France.
    Allerheiligenkapelle (stone), 12th c., Cathedral, Regensburg, Germany.

COSMIC CHRIST/PANTOCRATOR
47 Majestas Domini (ivory), Liège, early 11th c., Rouen Mus., France.
    Christ sending out the apostles to preach, 1120-50, Basilica of St Magdeleine, Vézelay, France.
    Noailles Gospels (book cover), late 10th c., Biblio. Nat., Paris.
    Ivory panel, c. 900, St. Mus., Berlin/Dahlem, Germany.
48 Godescalc Gospels, late 8th c., Biblio. Nat., Paris.
    Gallery capital, late 11th c., Church of St Sernin, Toulouse, France.
    Noailles Gospels (book cover), late 10th c., Biblio. Nat., Paris.
    Pantocrator, c.1349, Holy Apostles, Lesnovo, Yugoslavia.
49 Tympanum, late 12th c., Basle, Switzerland.
    Half-dome of apse (mosaic), 1148-75, Cefalù Cathedral, Sicily.
    Bust of the sun (stone relief of Visigothic period), c.700, Santa Maria de Quintanilla, Spain.
50 Dome (mosaic), 11th c., Church at Daphni, Greece.
    Dome (wall painting), 1349, Church of the Holy Archangels, Lesnovo, Yugoslavia.
    Dome (mosaic), 1140-54, Capella Palatina, Palermo, Sicily.
51 Stele (Georgian stone), 2nd half 6th c., Tbilisi Acad. of the Sciences Coll., Georgia, U.S.S.R.
    Ambulatory plaque, late 11th c., Church of St Sernin, Toulouse, France.
    Detail of Portail Royal, 1145-55, Chartres, France.
    Detail from apsidal painting at Bawît, late 6th c., Cairo Mus., Egypt.
52 Lorsch Gospels, c. 800, Bibl. Battyany, Alba Julia, Rumania.
    Diptych, 11th c., St. Bibliothek, Bamberg, Germany.
    Metz Sacramentary, Palace School of Charles the Bald, c. 870, Biblio. Nat. Paris.
    Ivory book cover, Liège, early 11th c., Bodleian Library, Oxford.
53 Metz Sacramentary, Palace School of Charles the Bald, c. 870, Biblio. Nat. Paris.
54 Dome (mosaic), 1140-54, Capella Palatina, Palermo, Sicily.

Dome (mosaic), 11th c., Church at Daphni, Greece.
Central portion of five-part diptych, mid-6th c., Marquet de Vaselot Coll.
Ivory panel, c. 900, St. Mus., Berlin/Dahlem, Germany.
55 Christ enthroned, flanked by St Vitale, Bishop Ecclesius and two angels, mid 6th c., S. Vitale, Ravenna, Italy.
Detail from apsidal painting at Bawît, late 6th c., Cairo Mus., Egypt.
56 West portal, c.1120, Cathedral of St Lazare, Autun, France.
Lorsch Gospels, c. 800, Bibl. Battyany, Alba Julia, Rumania.
Christ crowning SS Gereon and Victor (ivory), c.1000, Schnütgen Mus., Cologne, Germany.
Roger II crowned by Christ (mosaic), 1143-51, Martorana, Palermo, Sicily.
Lothair Gospels, Tours, mid-9th c., Biblio. Nat., Paris.

EASTER CYCLE: The Paschal Mystery/composite
57 Crucifixion (ivory), Cologne, c.1000, Mus. de Cluny, Paris.
Crucifixion and Resurrection, from Rabula Gospels, Syria, 586, Bibl. Laurenziana, Florence, Italy.
Resurrection and Ascension (ivory), N. Italy, c. 400, Bayerisches Nationalmus. Munich, Germany.
58 Scenes of the Passion (ivory), Rome, c. 430, British Museum, London.
Descent from the Cross, Entombment and Resurrection, Semokmedi icon (metal), 11th c., M.G.A., Tbilisi, U.S.S.R.
Resurrection and Ascension (ivory), N. Italy, c. 400, Bayerisches Nationalmus. Munich, Germany.
59 Crucifixion and Resurrection, from Rabula Gospels, Syria, 586, Bibl. Laurenziana, Florence, Italy.
60 Crucifixion (ivory), Cologne, c.1000, Mus. de Cluny, Paris.

EASTER CYCLE: Christ's glorious wounds
61 By Master H. E. (wood), 1511, Church at Kutna-Hora, Czechoslovakia.

EASTER CYCLE: Christ, Conqueror of Hell
62 Christ Pantocrator (ivory), late 8th c., Mus. Royaux d'Art et d'Histoire, Brussels.

EASTER CYCLE: The Harrowing of Hell
63 Book cover (silver gilt & cloisonné enamel), 12th c., St Mark's Treasury, Venice.
Mosaic, 11th c., Church at Daphni, Greece.
Martvili medallion (gold, enamel, pearls), 10th-11th c., (location not given.)
64 Mosaic, 11th c., Church at Daphni, Greece.

EASTER CYCLE: Doubting Thomas
65 Bas-relief, c.1100, Abbey of St Dominic, Silos, Spain.
Leaf of ivory diptych, St. Mus., Berlin/Dahlen, Germany.
Mosaic, 11th c., Church at Daphni, Greece.
66 Psalter of Blanche of Castile (miniature), c.1230, Bibl. de l'Arsenal, Paris.
67 Leaf of ivory diptych, St. Mus., Berlin/Dahlen, Germany.
Psalter of Blanche of Castile (miniature), c.1230, Bibl. de l'Arsenal, Paris.

EASTER CYCLE: Myrrh-Bearing Women at the Tomb
68 Reliquary lid (silver gilt), 12th c., Louvre, Paris.
Mosaic panel, c. 500, S. Apollinare Nuovo, Ravenna, Italy.
Ampulla for earth from the Holy Land, Monza, n.d.
69 Gospel-book No. 1796 (miniature), 12th c., Armenian Patriarchate, Jerusalem.
Psalter of Blanche of Castile (miniature), c.1230, Bibl. de l'Arsenal, Paris.
Reliquary lid (silver gilt), 12th c., Louvre, Paris.
Ampulla for earth from the Holy Land, Monza, n.d.
70 Antiphonal of St Peter's, Salzburg (miniature), Nationalbibliothek, Vienna.
Capital, early 12th c., Abbey of St Pierre, Mozat, France.
71 Gospel-book No. 1796 (miniature), 12th c., Armenian Patriarchate, Jerusalem.
Capital, early 12th c., Abbey of St Pierre, Mozat, France.

EASTER CYCLE: The Ascension
72 Rabula Gospels, Syria, 586, Biblioteca Laurenziana, Florence, Italy.
    Palace School of Charlemagne (ivory), c. 800, Landesmus., Darmstadt, Hesse, Germany.
    Casket lid, 11th c., Württembergisches Landesmus., Germany.
73 Icon, metalwork, 9th-11th c., Mus. of Georgian Art, Tbilisi, U.S.S.R.
    Palace School of Charlemagne (ivory), c. 800, Landesmus., Darmstadt, Hesse, Germany.
    Diptych from St George, Cologne (wood), c.1330-35, St. Mus., Berlin/Dahlem, Germany.
74 Rabula Gospels, Syria, 586, Biblioteca Laurenziana, Florence, Italy.
75 Plaque, 10th c., Bargello, Florence, Italy.
    Diptych from St George, Cologne (wood), c.1330-35, St. Mus., Berlin/Dahlem, Germany.
76 Metz Sacramentary, Palace School of Charles the Bald, c. 870, Biblio. Nat., Paris.
77 Ivory plaque from northern Italy, c. 400, Bayerisches Nationalmus., Munich, Germany.

EASTER CYCLE: Pentecost
79 Initial 'D' from Drogo Sacramentary, Metz, c. 580, Biblio. Nat., Paris.
    Missal of Abbot Berthold, Weingarten, 1200-32, Morgan Library, New York.

EXALTATION OF THE CROSS
80 Reliquary (silver gilt), Louvre, Paris.
    Container for relic of the True Cross (gold), c. 960, Cathedral Treasury, Limburg.
    Icon, 12th c., Tretyakov Gallery, Moscow.
    Center of five-part diptych, mid-6th c., Marquet de Vasselot Coll.
81 Processional cross (metal), 15th c., Daga Estifanos, Ethiopia.
    Silver plate discovered in the Crimea, c. 550, Hermitage, Leningrad.
    Cross of Justin II, 565-78, Vatican.
    Reliquary of the True Cross (cloisonné enamel), 11th c., Cathedral Treasury, Esztergom, Hungary.
82 Reliquary of the True Cross (cloisonné enamel), 11th c., Cathedral Treasury, Esztergom, Hungary.
    Container for relic of the True Cross (gold), c. 960, Cathedral Treasury, Limburg.
    Christ beneath archway, ampulla for earth from the Holy Land, Monza.
    Ivory diptych, mid-6th c., Matenadarak, Armenia, U.S.S.R.
83 Tympanum of west portal, Benedetto Antelami, 1196, Baptistery, Parma, Italy.
    Icon, 12th c., Tretyakov Gallery, Moscow.
    Cross beneath archway, ampulla for earth from the Holy Land, Monza.
    Triumph of Christ, ampulla for earth from the Holy Land, Monza.

FACE OF CHRIST
84 Wood, Massif Central, 12th c., Bresset Coll., La Rochelambert, Haute-Loire, France.
    Mosaic, c.1320, Kahrié, Cami, Istanbul.
    Works of the Metropolitan Jovan (wall painting), 1393-94, Skopje Art Gall., Yugoslavia.
    Icon (mosaic), c.1150, Bargello, Florence, Italy.
85 By Master Innerward (wood), after 1173, Brunswick Cathedral, Germany.
    Icon, 12th c., Tretyakov Gall., Moscow.
    Detail of fresco in apse, 1123, Church of St Clemente, Tahull, Spain.
    Wall painting, 14th c., Church at Ubisi, Georgia, U.S.S.R.
    Christ 'Saviour of Souls' (icon),14th c., Nat. Mus., Skopje, Yugoslavia.
    Icon (mosaic), c. 1150, Bargello, Florence, Italy.
    Detail of fresco in apse, 1123, Church of St Clemente, Tahull, Spain.
86 Wood, Massif Central, 12th c., Bresset Coll., La Rochelambert, Haute-Loire, France.
    Works of the Metropolitan Jovan (wall painting), 1393-94, Skopje Art Gall., Yugoslavia.
    Detail of mosaic, c. 900, S. Sophia, Istanbul (Constantinople).
    Coinage of Justinian II, 692-95, Dumbarton Oaks Coll., Washington.
    By Master Innerward (wood), after 1173, Brunswick Cathedral, Germany.
87 Icon, mid- or late 6th c., Monastery of St Catherine, Mount Sinai.
    Detail of mosaic, c. 900, S. Sophia, Istanbul (Constantinople).

Diptych, 11th c., St. Bibliothek, Bamberg, Germany.
88 Mosaic medallion, mid-6th c., S. Apollinare in Classe, Ravenna, Italy.
Icon, mid- or late 6th c., Monastery of St Catherine, Mount Sinai.
Detail of wall painting, c. 700 (?), Castelseprio (Lombardy), Italy.
Wall painting, 14th c., Church at Ubisi, Georgia, U.S.S.R.
89 Christ 'Saviour of Souls' (icon),14th c., Nat. Mus., Skopje, Yugoslavia.
Detail of wall painting, c. 700 (?), Castelseprio (Lombardy), Italy.
Coinage of Justinian II, 692-95, Dumbarton Oaks Coll., Washington.
Icon, mid- or late 6th c., Monastery of St Catherine, Mount Sinai.
Icon, 12th c., Tretyakov Gall., Moscow.

FOUR EVANGELISTS: Matthew
90 Canterbury Codex Aureus, mid-8th c., Kungliga Bibl., Stockholm.
Icon, 13th c., Nat. Mus., Ohrid, Yugoslavia.
Symbol of St Matthew, Book of Durrow, possibly from Iona, c. 680.
Illumination, Aachen, c. 800, Schatzkammer, Vienna.
91 Symbol of St Matthew, Book of Durrow, possibly from Iona, c. 680.
92 Lothair Gospels, Tours, c. 850, Biblio. Nat., Paris.
Shrine, lid, 12th c., Bargello, Florence, Italy.
Detail from Litchfield Gospels, early 8th c., Litchfield, England.
Illumination, Aachen, c. 800, Schatzkammer, Vienna.

FOUR EVANGELISTS: Mark
93 Symbol of St Mark, Book of Durrow, possibly from Iona, c. 680.
Detail from Litchfield Gospels, early 8th c., Litchfield, England.
Four Evangelists and Christ (mosaic border in apse), mid 6th c., S. Apollinare in Classe, Ravenna, Italy.

FOUR EVANGELISTS: Luke
94 Presbytery vault, S. Vitale, Ravenna, Italy.
So-called Gospels of St Augustine, 6th c., Corpus Christi College, Cambridge, England.
León Bible, 920.
Ebbo Gospels, early 9th c., Mun. Library, Epernay, France.
95 So-called Gospels of St Augustine, 6th c., Corpus Christi College, Cambridge, England.
96 León Bible, 920.
Detail from Litchfield Gospels, early 8th c., Litchfield, England.
Presbytery vault, S. Vitale, Ravenna, Italy.
Ebbo Gospels, early 9th c., Mun. Library, Epernay, France.
Casket, lid, 12th c., Bargello, Florence, Italy.

FOUR EVANGELISTS: John
97 Coronation Sacramentary, Aachen, Germany, c. 800, Schatzkammer, Vienna.
Icon, 14th c., Mus. of the Monastery of Chiliándari, Mount Athos, Greece.
Symbol of St John, Book of Dimma, 8th c., Trinity College, Dublin.
Shroud of St Germain (silk), late 10th c., St Eusèbe, Auxerre, France.
98 Symbol of St John, Book of Dimma, 8th c., Trinity College, Dublin.
Detail from Litchfield Gospels, early 8th c., Litchfield, England.
Icon, 14th c., Mus. of the Monastery of Chiliándari, Mount Athos, Greece.

GOSPEL SCENES: Lazarus/Woman at the Well
99 Miniature painted by Toros Roslin (Gospel-book No. 10675), 1268, Yerevan, Armenia.
Detail of Raising of Lazarus, 12th c., Victoria & Albert Museum, London.
Silver reliquary, c. 600, Louvre, Paris.
Details of five-part diptych, mid-6th c., Biblio. Nat., Paris.

GOSPEL SCENES: Woman at the Well, cont'd/Healing of the Blind Man
100 Christ and the Woman of Samaria, mid-6th c., Archiepiscopal Mus., Ravenna.
    Healing of a blind man (marble relief from Istanbul), c. 400, Dumbarton Oaks Coll., Washington.

GOSPEL SCENES: Miracles: Baptismal Catechesis
101 Christian sarcophagus, c. 330, Nat. Mus., Rome.
    Christian sarcophagus, 1st half of 4th c., Mus. Pio Cristiano, Vatican.
    Christian sarcophagus (Adam & Eve, Miracles of Christ, Adoration of Magi, New Adam, Betrayal of Peter?), c. 320-30, Mus. Pio Cristiano, Vatican.

HEBREW PROPHETS: Isaiah, Ezekiel, David, Moses
102 Isaiah (relief on portal), c.1107-17, Cathedral, Cremona, Italy.
    Isaiah (bas-relief), 1130-40, Church of St Marie, Souillac, France.
    King David, late 11th c., Portico de los Orfebres, Cathedral, Santiago de Compostella, Spain.
    Ezekiel, early 12th c., Cathedral, Borgo San Donino, Italy.
103 Isaiah (relief on portal), c.1107-17, Cathedral, Cremona, Italy.
    Moses receiving the Tables of the Law (ivory), St. Mus., Berlin/Dahlen.
    King David, late 11th c., Portico de los Orfebres, Cathedral, Santiago de Compostella, Spain.

LAMB OF GOD
104 Triumph of the Lamb (mosaic), St Vitale, Ravenna, Italy.
    Triumphal cross known as the Cross of Justin II, 565-78, Vatican.
    Ravenna-style sarcophagus, late 5th c., St Vitale, Ravenna.

LAST JUDGEMENT
105 English ivory, 10th c., Victoria and Albert Mus., London.
    Apocalyptic scene from Beatus Vit. 14-I, 10th c., Bibl. Nac., Madrid.
    Allegory of the Last Judgement, c. 500, St Apollinare Nuovo, Ravenna.
    Weighing of souls, Maser of Soriguela (painted wood), late 13th c., Catalan Mus. of Art, Barcelona.
    Hanged man tormented by devils (capital), late 11th c., Cathedral, Santiago de Compostella, Spain.

LIFE OF THE VIRGIN MARY
106 Presentation of the Virgin in the Temple (mosaic), 11th c., Church at Daphni, Greece.
    Visitation, from Wimpfen, Austria (stained glass), c.1270-80, Hessisches Landesmus., Darmstadt, Germany.
    Birth of the Virgin (mosaic), 11th c., Church at Daphni, Greece.

MARY, MOTHER OF GOD / "THEOTOKOS"
107 Virgin and Child with the donor Turtura (wall painting), 528, Catacomb of Commodilla, Rome.
    Apse decoration, mid-6th c., Basilica Euphrasiana, Porec, Istria, Yugoslavia.
108 Polyptych (polychrome ivory), early 14th c., Victoria and Albert Museum, London.
109 Polyptych (polychrome ivory), early 14th c., Victoria and Albert Museum, London.
    Noailles Gospels (ivory book cover), late 10th c., Biblio. Nat., Paris.
110 Lorsch Gospels (book cover), c. 800, Victoria and Albert Museum, London.
    Noailles Gospels (ivory book cover), late 10th c., Biblio. Nat., Paris.
    Icon, 13th c., Monastery of St Catherine, Mount Sinai.
    Ivory, 11th c., Archiepiscopal Mus., Utrecht, Netherlands.
111 Icon, Nat. Mus., Ohrid, Yugoslavia.
    Icon, c. 600, Monastery of St Catherine, Mount Sinai.
    Icon, 13th-14th c., Crypt of St Alexander Nevsky, Sofia, Bulgaria.
    Triptych (bronze), 12th c., Victoria and Albert Museum, London.
    Apse mosaic, 14th c. (?), Church at Murano, Italy.
112 Virgin and Child with the donor Turtura (wall painting), 528, Catacomb of Commodilla, Rome.
    Icon, Nat. Mus., Ohrid, Yugoslavia.
    Icon known as the Virgin of Vladimir, c.1130, Tretyakov Gallery, Moscow.
    Ivory, 11th c., Archiepiscopal Mus., Utrecht, Netherlands.

Statuette, 10th c., Victoria and Albert Museum, London.
113 Icon, c. 600, Monastery of St Catherine, Mount Sinai.
   The Theotokos Aniketos (marble bas-relief), 13th c., St Mark, Venice.
   Icon, Virgin of Pimen, 14th c., Tretyakov Gallery, Moscow.
   Virgin and Child with the donor Turtura (wall painting), 528, Catacomb of Commodilla, Rome.
   Apse decoration, mid 6th c., Basilica Euphrasiana, Porec, Istria, Yugoslavia.
114 Icon, 13th c., Monastery of St Catherine, Mount Sinai.
   Icon known as the Virgin of Vladimir, c. 1130, Tretyakov Gallery, Moscow.
   Lorsch Gospels (book cover), c. 800, Victoria and Albert Museum, London.
   Icon, 13th-14th c., Crypt of St Alexander Nevsky, Sofia, Bulgaria.
   Detail from The Virgin flanked by the Emperor John Comnenus and the Empress Irene (mosaic), c. 1118, Istanbul.
115 Virgin of Bishop Imad (wood), 1050-60, Diözesanmus., Paderborn, Germany.
   Tympanum of right portal, west front, 1165-70, Cathedral of Notre Dame, Paris.
   Virgin of Mösjo, Sweden (polychrome wood), mid-12th c., Hist. Mus., Stockholm.
   Tympanum of right portal, north front, 2nd half of 12th c., Cathedral, Reims, France.
   Virgin from Massif Central (polychrome wood), 12th c., Mus. at Nancy, France.
   Our Lady of Good Hope (polychrome wood), 3rd quarter 12th c., Church of Notre Dame, Dijon, France.
116 Tympanum of right portal, west front, 1165-70, Cathedral of Notre Dame, Paris.
   Wood engraving from Upper Rhine, Germany, c.1420, Biblio. Nat., Paris.
   Virgin by Nino Pisano (stone), 1343-47, S. Maria della Spina, Pisa, Italy.
117 Virgin of Mösjo, Sweden (polychrome wood), mid-12th c., Hist. Mus., Stockholm.
   Virgin from Catalonia (gesso and cloth on wood), 12th c., Church in Montserrat, Spain.
118 Virgin from Massif Central (polychrome wood), 12th c., Mus. at Nancy, France.
   Our Lady of Good Hope (polychrome wood), 3rd quarter 12th c., Church of Notre Dame, Dijon, France.
   Tympanum of right portal, north front, 2nd half of 12th c., Cathedral, Reims, France.
119 Portal (limestone), last quarter 14th c., Champmol, France.
   Virgin from Wroclaw, Poland (polychrome stone), c.1400, Nat. Mus., Warsaw.
   Virgin from Krumlov, Czechoslovakia (stone), c.1400, Kunsthistorisches Mus., Vienna.
   Virgin formerly at St John of the Virgin, Torun, Poland (stone), late 14th c.
120 Virgin by Adriaen van Wesel (polychrome wood), 1470-80, Rijksmus., Amsterdam.
   Virgin from Wroclaw, Poland (polychrome stone), c.1400, Nat. Mus., Warsaw.
   Virgin formerly at St John of the Virgin, Torun, Poland (stone), late 14th c.
   Portal (limestone), last quarter 14th c., Champmol, France.

PASSION CYCLE: Entry into Jerusalem
121 Plaque, 10th c., St. Mus., Berlin/Dahlen.
   Mosaic, 11th c., Church at Daphni, Greece.
   Mosaic, 1315, Holy Apostles, Salonica, Greece.
122 Mosaic, 1315, Holy Apostles, Salonica, Greece.
   Mosaic, 11th c., Church at Daphni, Greece.

PASSION CYCLE: Last Supper: Communion of the Apostles
123 Ambulatory capital, mid-12th c., Church of St Paul, Issoire, France.
   Epitaphion (embroidery), 14th c., Benaki Museum, Athens.
124 Ambulatory capital, mid-12th c., Church of St Paul, Issoire, France.
   Mosaic, 11th c., Panagia Chalkeon, Salonica, Greece.

PASSION CYCLE: Foot Washing
125 Mosaic, 11th c., Church at Daphni, Greece.
   Wall painting, 1312, Church, Monastery of Vatopédi, Mount Athos, Greece.

PASSION CYCLE: Gethsemane
126 Wall painting, 14th c., S. Nicholas, Curtea de Arges, Rumania.
   Mosaic panel, c. 500, S. Apollinare Nuovo, Ravenna, Italy.

PASSION CYCLE: Trial
127 Three scenes from Christian sarcophagus, c. 350, Mus. Pio Cristiano, Vatican.
   The Crowning with Thorns (stained glass), c. 1250, Sainte-Chapelle, Paris.

PASSION CYCLE: Christ Carrying his Cross
128 Wood, c.1420-30, S. Thiébaut, Thann, France.
   Scene from Christian sarcophagus, c. 350, Mus. Pio Cristiano, Vatican.
   Ivory, Rome, c. 430, British Museum, London.
   Heures de Jeanne d'Evreux (miniature), 1322-28, Biblio. Nat., Paris.
   Christian sarcophagus with scenes of Christ's Passion, c. 350, Mus. Pio Cristiano, Vatican.
129 Heures de Jeanne d'Evreux (miniature), 1322-28, Biblio. Nat., Paris.
   Wood, c.1420-30, S. Thiébaut, Thann, France.

PASSION CYCLE: Crucifixion
130 Ivory panel of Bishop Adalbéron, c. 1005, Mus. Mus., Metz, Germany.
131 Ivory from Rome, c. 430, British Museum, London.
   Codex Aureus, Trier (ivory book cover), early 11th c., Nationalmus., Nürenberg, Germany.
   Box reliquary of the Holy Cross (silver), 11th-12th c., Hermitage Mus., Leningrad.
   Crucifixion from St George, Cologne (wood), mid-11th c., Schnütgen Mus., Cologne.
   Panel on altar frontal, c. 1084, Mus. del Duomo, Salerno, Sicily.
132 Plaque from Athlone (bronze gilt), 8th c., Nat. Mus., Dublin.
   Ivory panel, Liège, late 10th c., Mus. Notre-Dame, Tongres, Belgium.
   Central compartment of triptych, c. 988, British Museum, London.
   Codex Aureus, Trier (ivory book cover), early 11th c., Nationalmus., Nürenberg, Germany.
133 Diptych from St George, Cologne (wood, painted and gilt), c.1330-35, St. Mus., Berlin/Dahlem.
   Mosaic, 11th c., Church at Daphni, Greece.
   Box reliquary of the Holy Cross (silver), 11th-12th c., Hermitage Mus., Leningrad.
   Miniature, Cod. gr. 74, 11th c., Biblio. Nat., Paris.
134 Crucifixion with donors, Cologne (stained glass), c. 1313, Hessisches Landesmus., Darmstadt, Germany.
   Southampton Psalter, c. 1000, St John's College, Cambridge, England.
   Medallion, west front (stained glass), 1150-55, Cathedral, Chartres, France.
   Miniature, Cod. gr. 74, 11th c., Biblio. Nat., Paris.
   Ivory panel of Bishop Adalbéron, c. 1005, Mus. Mus., Metz, Germany.
135 Duvillaun stele, 8th c., Ireland.
   Crucifix (wood), c. 1460, St Bartholomew, Plzen, Czechoslovakia.
   Crucifixion from Massif Central (polychrome wood), 12th c., Church in Arlet, Haute-Loire, France.
   Medallion, west front (stained glass), 1150-55, Cathedral, Chartres, France.
   Crucifixion with donors, Cologne (stained glass), c. 1313, Hessisches Landesmus., Darmstadt, Germany.
136 Ambo by Nicolas of Verdun (enamelled plaquette), 1181, Klosterneuburg, Austria.
   Crucifixion from Massif Central (polychrome wood), 12th c., Church in Arlet, Haute-Loire, France.
   Initial 'T' from Gellone Sacramentary, late 8th c., Biblio. Nat., Paris.
   Ivory panel, Liège, late 10th c., Mus. Notre-Dame, Tongres, Belgium.
   Reliquary medallion of the Cross (gold and cloisonné enamel), 11th c., Armoury, Kremlin, Moscow, U.S.S.R.
137 Initial 'T' from Gellone Sacramentary, late 8th c., Biblio. Nat., Paris.
   Crucifix (walnut), c. 1400, St George, Cologne, Germany.
   Reliquary cross (ivory, gold and enamels), late 10th c., Victoria and Albert Mus., London.
   Crucifix (wood), c. 1460, St Bartholomew, Plzen, Czechoslovakia.
138 Central compartment of triptych, c. 988, British Museum, London.
   Polychrome wood, Tyrol, late 12th c., Innsbruck Mus., Austria.
   Manuscript of the Four Gospels, VI, 23, Biblioteca Laurenziana, Florence, Italy.
   Cross, c. 800, South of Clonmacnoise, Ireland.
139 Panel on altar frontal, c. 1084, Mus. del Duomo, Salerno, Sicily.
   Moone Cross, 8th c., Kildare, Ireland.
   Mosaic, 11th c., Church at Daphni, Greece.
   Crucifixion from St George, Cologne (wood), mid-11th c., Schnütgen Mus., Cologne.

140 Codex Aureus, Trier (ivory book cover), early 11th c., Nationalmus., Nürenberg, Germany.
Polychrome wood, Tyrol, late 12th c., Innsbruck Mus., Austria.
Crucifix of King Ferdinand I, León, St Isidoro, 1063, Mus. Arqueol., Madrid.
Duvillaun stele, 8th c., Ireland.
141 Southampton Psalter, c. 1000, St John's College, Cambridge, England.
Manuscript of the Four Gospels, VI, 23, Biblioteca Laurenziana, Florence, Italy.
Muiredach Cross, c. 900, Monasterboice, Ireland.

PASSION CYCLE: Descent from the Cross
142 Book cover, Herefordshire, c. 1150, Victoria and Albert Mus., London.
Wall painting, 1164, St Panteleimon, Nerezi, Yugoslavia.
Wall painting, 1282, Omorphoklissia, Aegina, Greece.
Miniature, Dzruci Gospels, 12th c., Tbilisi, Georgia, U.S.S.R.
143 Wall painting, 1282, Omorphoklissia, Aegina, Greece.
Book cover, Herefordshire, c. 1150, Victoria and Albert Mus., London.
Miniature, Gelati Gospels, 12th c., Institute for the Conservation of Manuscripts, Tbilisi, Georgia, U.S.S.R.

PASSION CYCLE: Burial
144 Epitaphion (embroidery), 1407, Victoria and Albert Mus., London.
Entombment (stone), 1515, Bayon church, France.
Detail of Epitaphion (from top of page).

PASSION CYCLE: Pieta
145 Stone, c. 1420, Church of Our Lady, Maastricht, Netherlands.
Stone, from Seeon Abbey, 1410-20, Bayerisches Nationalmus., Munich, Germany.
146 Limestone, c. 1385, St Thomas, Brno, Czechoslovakia.
Walnut, from Middle Rhine, early 15th c., Liebighaus, Frankfurt, Germany.
147 Stone, from Seeon Abbey, 1410-20, Bayerisches Nationalmus., Munich, Germany.
Walnut, from Middle Rhine, early 15th c., Liebighaus, Frankfurt, Germany.
148 Stone, c. 1400, St Lambert, Düsseldorf, Germany.
Stone, c. 1420, Church of Our Lady, Maastricht, Netherlands.

PRESENTATION OF THE LORD
149 Icon, metalwork, 9th-11th c., Mus. of Georgian Art, Tbilisi, Georgia, U.S.S.R.
Icon, enamel on gold ground, 12th-13th c., Mus. of Georgian Art, Tbilisi, Georgia, U.S.S.R.
Detail, west front, early 13th c., Cathedral, Borgo San Donino, Italy.
150 Mosaic, 11th c., Principal church, Monastery of H. Loukas, Phokis, Greece.
Fresco by Giotto, 1304-05, Scrovegni Chapel, Padua, Italy.
Wall painting, 10th c., St John, Güllü deré, Cappadocia.
151 Fresco by Giotto, 1304-05, Scrovegni Chapel, Padua, Italy.
Detail, west front, early 13th c., Cathedral, Borgo San Donino, Italy.

SAINTS: John the Baptist
152 St John the Baptist with apostles (plaque), 11th c., Victoria and Albert Mus., London.
Head of St John, from the Lower Rhine (limestone), early 16th c., Schnütgen Mus., Cologne, Germany
Leaf of diptych of Bishop Grandison (ivory), mid-14th c., British Museum, London.

SAINTS: Stephen the Martyr
153 Votive painting, 7th c., Catacomb of Commodilla, Rome.
Wall painting, mid-9th c., St Germain d'Auxerre, France.

SAINTS: Nicholas, George, Gregory the Wonderworker & Demitrius
154 St Demetrius (icon, soapstone), 11th c., Kremlin Mus., U.S.S.R.
St Nicholas (icon), 12th-13th c., Tretyakov Gall., Moscow, U.S.S.R.
St Gregory the Wonderworker (mosaic), 11th c., Church at Daphni, Greece.

St George slaying the dragon (icon), 14th c., Tretyakov Gall., Moscow, U.S.S.R.

SAINTS: Gregory the Great, Dorothy, Martin & King David
155 Inspiration of St Gregory by the Holy Spirit (ivory book cover), late 10th c., Kunsthistorisches Mus., Vienna.
   St Dorothy, from Middle Rhine (stained glass), c. 1480, Hessisches Landesmus., Darmstadt, Germany.
   Charity of St Martin, by Andrea and Nino Pisano (stone), mid-14th c., St Martino, Pisa, Italy.
   King David, from Wimpfen, Austria (stained glass), c. 1270-80, Hessisches Landesmus., Darmstadt, Germany.

TRANSFIGURATION OF OUR LORD
156 Mosaic, 11th c., Church at Daphni, Greece.
   Apse mosaic, mid-6th c., Monastery of St Catherine, Mount Sinai.
   Carved ivory panel, c. 800, Victoria and Albert Mus., London.
   Plaque, 12th c., Victoria and Albert Mus., London.
157 Carved ivory panel, c. 800, Victoria and Albert Mus., London.
   Plaque, 12th c., Victoria and Albert Mus., London.
   Apse mosaic, mid-6th c., Monastery of St Catherine, Mount Sinai.

TRINITY
158 Abraham and the Three Angels (Ingeborg Psalter), 1193-1213, Mus. Condé, Chantilly, France.
   Hospitality of Abraham (Icon), 14th c., Byzantine Mus., Athens.
159 Icon, painted by Andrei Rublev, 1411, Tretyakov Gall., Moscow.
160 The Ancient of Days (wall painting), 14th c., Church at Ubisi, Georgia, U.S.S.R.
   Trinity, by T. Riemenschneider (limewood), c. 1516, St. Mus., Berlin/Dahlem.

SOURCES
   Title: Detail from a portable altar, Adelshausen, c. 800, Augustinermus., Freiburg im Bresgau, Germany.
   Endpiece: Nave capital; foliate decoration, 1st half of the 12th cen., Collegiate Church of S. Andoche, Saulieu, France.

BACK COVER
   Ottonian book cover, ivory, in the Carolingian style, early 11th cen., Mus. Royaux d'Art et d'Histoire, Brussels.

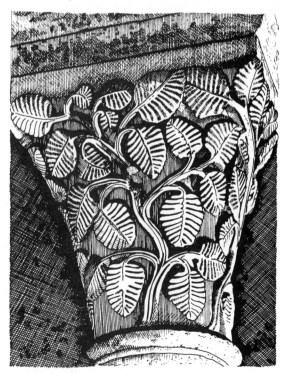

ACKNOWLEDGEMENTS

(Many of the extracts presented here were copied in the course of reading over twenty five years; I am grateful to the authors and publishers below as well as to those named in the text. I regret I have not been able to provide full references for all of them.)

All scripture citations (with the exception of the the the Psalms, which are the editor's renderings): *The New English Bible with the Apocrypha* (Oxford U. P. & Cambridge U. P., 1970), and *The Jerusalem Bible* (London, Darton, Longman and Todd, 1966); pages 21, 25, 65, 73, 77, 81, 115, 117, 119, 125, 127, 143, 144, 149, 157: *The Dayspring Hymnal* (Hermitage of the Dayspring, Kent, CT 06757, unpublished); 8, 13, 24, 26, 51, 96, 99: *The Divine Office: The Liturgy of the Hours according to the Roman Rite,* 3 vols. (London, Collins 1974); 134, 145: *The Missal in Latin and English* (London, Burns Oates and Washbourne, 1958); 18, 62, 82, 105, 147, 159: *The Oxford Book of Prayer,* ed. George Appleton (Oxford, Oxford University Press, 1985); 16, 35, 37, 61, 68, 92, 106, 123, 124, 130, 136: *The Rites of the Catholic Church,* 2 volumes (New York, Pueblo Publishing Co.), 1976-1980; 47, 86, 122, 129, 139, 142: *The Roman Sacramentary* (Collegeville, MN, Liturgical Press, 1974).

Page 89: St AELRED of Rievaulx, *The Mirror of Charity,* trans. Geoffrey Webb & Adrian Walker (London, Catholic Book Club, 1962); 141: St ANDREW OF CRETE, *The Great Canon* (Whitby, UK, Greek Orthodox Monastery of the Assumption, 1974); 3: William BLAKE, quoted in Theodore Rosak, *Making of a Counter Culture*; 31, 94: Raymond E. BROWN: *The Birth of the Messiah* (Garden City, NY, Doubleday, 1977; 128, 137, 148, 160: Petru DUMITRIU: *To The Unknown God* (NY, Seabury, 1982); 14: Abraham Joshua HESCHEL: *Reflections on Death* (essay); 57, 153: Gerard Manley HOPKINS: *Poems,* 4th ed. London, Oxford University Press, 1970; 107, 109, 111: Caryll HOUSELANDER, *The Reed of God* (Westminster, MD, Christian Classics, 1985); 27, 66, 126: JUNG and LAVELLE, from May Sarton: *Journal of a Solitude* (New York, W. W. Norton, 1973); 71: Madeleine L'ENGLE, *The Irrational Season* (NY, Seabury, 1977); 30: Henry MILLER, from William Least Heat Moon, *Blue Highways*; 102: Alexander SCHMEMANN, *Of Water and The Spirit* (Crestwood, NY, St. Vladimir's Seminary Press, 1974); 70: John SHEA, from a poem called *The Resurrection Prayers of Magdalene, Peter, and Two Youths*; 155: Staretz SILOUAN, *Wisdom from Mount Athos,* ed. Archimandrite Sophrony (Crestwood, NY, St. Vladimir's Seminary Press, 1974); 85, 127: John SOBRINO, S.J., *Christology at the Crossroads* (Maryknoll, NY, Orbis Books, 1978); 2, 7, 29: Karl STERN: *The Pillar of Fire* (New York, Harcourt, Brace, 1957), and *Flight From Woman*; 80: Gerardus VAN DER LEEUW, *Sacred and Profane Beauty;* 72: Damasus WINZEN, unpublished conference; 102: *Pathways in Scripture (*Ann Arbor, MI, Servant Books, 1976); 104: Alexander (Y)ELCHANINOV, *The Diary of a Russian Priest* (London, Faber and Faber, 1967).